The Changing World of the Executive

Peter F. Drucker

Harvard Business Press

Boston, Massachusetts

Copyright 2010 Harvard Business School Publishing Corporation

All rights reserved

Printed in the United States of America

14 13 12 11 10   5 4 3 2 1

No part of this publication may be reproduced, stored in or introduced into a retrieval system, or transmitted, in any form, or by any means (electronic, mechanical, photocopying, recording, or otherwise), without the prior permission of the publisher. Requests for permission should be directed to permissions@hbsp.harvard.edu, or mailed to Permissions, Harvard Business School Publishing, 60 Harvard Way, Boston, Massachusetts 02163.

ISBN: 978-1-4221-3156-5
Library-of-Congress cataloging information forthcoming

The paper used in this publication meets the requirements of the American National Standard for Permanence of Paper for Publications and Documents in Libraries and Archives Z39.48-1992.

CONTENTS

INTRODUCTION: A SOCIETY

OF ORGANIZATIONS

SOCIETY in this century has become a society of organizations. Social tasks which only a century ago were done by the family, in the home, in the shop, or on the farm—from providing goods and services to education and care of the sick and the elderly—are increasingly performed in and through large organizations. These organizations—whether business enterprises, hospitals, schools, or universities—are designed for continuity and run by professional managers. Executives have thus become the leadership groups in our society. The leadership groups of old—whether nobles, priests, landed aristocracy, or business tycoons—have disappeared or become peripheral.

The first job of the executive is to make his organization perform. Results are always on the outside. There are only costs on the inside. Even the most efficient manufacturing plant is still a cost center until a distant customer has paid for its products. The executive thus lives in a constant struggle to keep performance from being overtaken by the concerns of the inside, that is, by bureaucracy. Business at least stands under the control of the market, which forces even the most powerful corporation to subordinate its inside concerns to outside results and to performance. But in the public service institution, where the market test is absent—and in many cases cannot even be simulated—bureaucracy constantly threatens to swallow up performance.

For the business enterprise in a market system we are gradually developing a discipline of entrepreneurship, that is, of performance.

But even the President of the United States fights a losing battle to preserve his capacity to give political leadership and to make political decisions in the face of the need to manage an unmanageably large, unmanageably complex, and self-centered bureaucratic machine.

The art and discipline of entrepreneurship to make organizations perform and to produce results will therefore be a continuing concern. This concern will involve the public service institution as well as the business enterprise.

The executive as a person—as a key individual in society and as a member of his organization—becomes a matter of increasing importance. Middle managers and other professionals working as individual contributors—as engineers, as chemists, as accountants, as computer programers, as medical technologists, and so on—have constituted the fastest-growing group in American society, and indeed in the society of all developed countries. Careers in organizations—that is, careers as managers and other professionals—are the principal career opportunities for educated people. Nine out of ten youngsters who receive a college degree can expect to spend all their working lives as managerial or other professional employees of institutions.

Social theorists and political scientists still, by and large, divide the world into "bosses" and "working stiffs." But this was the reality of the nineteenth century. The reality of today consists of people who are "bosses" but who also have bosses of their own; who are not "capitalists" but who collectively—through their pension funds and their savings—own the economy; people who consider themselves "professionals" but who are also "employees" as "professionals" traditionally were not supposed to be.

Who are they? What do they represent? Where do they stand? What are their problems, their opportunities, their concerns? How can they best use their organizations to achieve their own ends in life and work? And what, in turn, do they owe the organizations that enable them to live comfortable, well-paid, middle-class lives by furnishing the capital they themselves lack and by taking the risks that they could not afford or dare to take themselves?

There are, of course, many other concerns of management and manager: the impact of new technology, labor relations, government regulation, and growing worldwide economic integration; taxation and compensation; rapidly changing internal organization; and the development of managers.

There is the curious ambivalence in our society that shows an apparently hostile face to business and to large organizations but that also favors business schools to the extent that they have become the fastest-growing institutions of higher education. Indeed, the Master of Business Administration degree has become increasingly important for advancement in public service organizations as well as in businesses.

There is the changing age structure of society, which for the young adult is creating a climate of extreme competition. And increasingly, too, there is the desire for a second career for the middle-aged manager and professional—a problem for the individual and a challenge to the organization that employs him.

Despite all the outpouring of management writing these last twenty-five years, the world of management is still little-explored. It is a world of issues, but also a world of people. And it is undergoing rapid change right now.

These essays explore a wide variety of topics. They deal with changes in the work force, its jobs, its expectations, with the power relationships of a "society of employees," and with changes in technology and in the world economy. They discuss the problems and challenges facing major institutions, including business enterprises, schools, hospitals, and government agencies. They look anew at the tasks and work of executives, at their performance and its measurement, and at executive compensation.

However diverse the topics, all the pieces reflect upon the same reality: In all developed countries the workaday world has become a "society of organizations" and thus dependent on executives, that is, on people—whether called managers or administrators—who are paid to direct organizations and to make them perform. These chapters have one common theme: the changing world of the executive—changing rapidly within the organization; changing rapidly in respect to the visions, aspirations, and even characteristics of employees, customers, and constituents; changing outside the organization as well—economically, technologically, socially, politically.

Of the more than three dozen chapters in this volume, thirty-nine appeared first on the editorial page of *The Wall Street Journal*, one—chapter 23, "The Professor as Featherbedder"—first appeared in the *Chronicle of Higher Education*, and the final chapter, "The Matter of 'Business Ethics'" was originally written for *The Public Interest* and published there.

This book has two aims. One is to give insight into—and an understanding of—this world of the executive. The second is to provide a useful "executive agenda." Modern organization, as we now know it, is barely one hundred years old. It did not become conceptually visible and an object of study until World War II—less than half a century ago. This new continent has been named and its outlines can be delineated. But otherwise we are still in a fairly early stage of its exploration. My second aim for this book, as an executive agenda, is to stimulate both thought and action and to be read with this overriding question in mind: "How can I, and we in my organization, use this idea or these insights to perform more effectively—to do a better job and, above all, to welcome and accommodate the new and the different?"

Peter F. Drucker
Claremont, California
Thanksgiving Day, 1981

PART I

Executive Agenda

Management texts stress managing others. Few talk of managing oneself. But managing others is always "iffy." Does it really work? One can, however, always manage oneself, or at least try.

Managing others is most effectively done by example rather than by preaching or policy. If the example is lacking, the most moving sermon and the wisest policy rarely work. "Do as I tell you and not as I do" is the motto of the outsider, the consultant. Effective executives know that their associates will do as the boss does, and not necessarily as the boss says.

Hence the first section of this volume on the executive and his changing world appropriately deals with the executive, his or her performance, his or her tasks and roles. And since executives are paid to perform and to make sure the right things are done, a keynote is sounded in the second chapter by a piece on managerial performance and its measurement and on the organized feedback needed for continuous learning and self-development in an executive.

CHAPTER ONE

Inflation-Proofing the Company

EVERY WEEK, IT SEEMS, another book comes out announcing the one sure way to protect the individual and his money against inflation. But no one seems to pay much attention to protecting business. And yet little individual wealth is likely to survive unless the economy's wealth-generating assets, its businesses, retain their capacity to produce. And that this capacity is endangered by prolonged inflation—let alone by chronic inflation at high rates such as the whole world is now experiencing—everyone accepts, including even the "progressive" economists for whom inflation is very much the lesser evil.

It is impossible for a business—and indeed for an individual as well—to acquire total immunity against the ravages of inflation. But it is possible to "inflation-proof" a business so as to give it both a fair degree of resistance against the pandemic disease and the power to recover. And it can be done quite cheaply and with moderate efforts.

The first thing to do—indeed the absolute prerequisite—is to get the facts. A business that does not adjust its figures to inflation—and only a few big companies are so far doing so in the U.S.—cannot fight inflation but becomes its victim. It is bound to do things that greatly increase inflation's damage for the simple reason that it bases its decisions on misinformation and self-delusion. Without inflation-adjusted accounting, businesses must believe that their sales go up when in effect both sales and market standing go down. They must believe that they are making record profits when, in effect, profitability goes down or disappears entirely. They must believe that they are financially strong when, in effect, they are on the brink of insolvency and have no power of resistance against "credit crunch" and "liquidity crisis"—both endemic in an inflationary period. Sales and market standing; receivables and inventory; depreciation, capital, and debt-service requirements; and profits need to be restated continuously in inflation-adjusted figures to enable the business to inflation-proof itself.

The next step is systematic money management. One of the inevitable distortions of an inflationary period is overemphasis on finance. Manipulating money comes to be seen as more important than making and marketing goods or services when, with interest rates at 17 percent, an inept or inexperienced treasurer can lose the firm more money in a week than marketing can make in three months. But to inflation-proof a company more is needed than clever manipulation of cash and speculation in interest rates (though both, alas, are needed in inflationary times). The business has to be managed to satisfy at the same time two essentially incompatible requirements. It has to have minimum exposure to loss through the depreciation of the currency, which implies having the minimum of cash and the maximum of short-term debt. But at the same time an inflationary period demands a high degree of liquidity. In any inflationary period sudden attacks of "liquidity crisis" and "credit crunch" will occur without any warning. And contrary to what all politicians promise, there is no "soft landing" after inflationary bouts—at least there has been none in any of the attacks of inflation in modern economic history since the first one, the hundred-plus years of steady worldwide and corrosive inflation in the sixteenth century.

To inflation-proof a business thus requires a careful, principled, long-range policy of balance between the risk of loss from too much liquidity and the risk of catastrophe from too little. How high a risk premium does *this* company with its own specific financial characteristics have to pay to be able to ride out a liquidity crisis or a credit crunch? The financial panics of an inflationary period can be likened to a September hurricane in the Caribbean: They blow themselves out fast as a rule. But that is scant comfort if the boat has turned over and sunk at the first hard blow.

And finally, inflation-proofing the business requires deliberate contempt for the madness that in an inflationary period passes for sanity: the focus on the very short and the immediate. This focus is "rational" in an inflationary period. For with an interest rate of 17 percent or so, nothing further away than four years has any present value at all—and if there is any risk at all, the timespan beyond which investments in the future shrink to a present value of zero goes down to two years or so. This means that it becomes "rational" in an inflationary period to forgo any expenditure returns for which are both less than "certain" and a few years away. It becomes "rational" to rob the future. But as we were reminded by the environmental crisis a few years back, this is not "rationality" but madness, and the most wasteful and expensive thing conceivable.

In every inflation since the sixteenth century the "smart boys" managed short-term. They always were the "miracle workers" and the "hot pistols" for a while. But the moment the inflation stopped—or even paused—they always crashed in flames. The "magician" of the German hyperinflation of the twenties was a certain Hugo Stinnes, who, in three feverish years, built what was then Europe's largest and apparently most powerful "conglomerate." Six months after the German mark had been stabilized in October 1923, Stinnes was bankrupt and his empire in liquidation.

The ones who survive are the "dumb" ones who prepare for the future. The best example is again a German one—Siemens. During the German inflation Siemens was considered "hopeless." But the company emerged as the world's number-two electrical apparatus giant (second only to America's GE). Its old European rival, the (also German) AEG, was "smart" during the inflation and the darling of securities analysts and financial writers; it has never recovered its competitive strength but has been slipping further and further behind ever since. And what Siemens did was quite simple. Its day-to-day operation, including money management, was run in accordance with the reality of inflation. Everything to do with the making of tomorrow was run as if inflation did not exist.

To inflation-proof the business, the activities that make tomorrow—scientific and technical research, product and process innovation and development; maintenance of plant and equipment; market development; customer service; and the development and training of professional, managerial, and skilled people—are run as if the interest rate were 3 percent, that is with disregard for the inflation charge. These activities account for at least one tenth of total expenditures in any business—in some they account for much more. But to inflation-proof the business they must be given priority over everything, with the exception of the cash flow necessary to protect the business against the pressures of the liquidity crunch.

And incidentally, maintaining their own "wealth-producing capacity," that is their skill and knowledge, may be the best way for individuals to make themselves inflation-proof. History makes one doubt all and any of the clever schemes to beat inflation—whether investing in real estate or in diamonds, in commodities, in gold or in antiques—which today's best-selling books so persuasively promote. Governments have somehow always found ways to get the better of the cleverest inflation-beating scheme. But while the German farmers, shopkeepers, and industrialists had still not recovered ten years later from the inflation of 1920 to 1923—a major factor, of course, in Hitler's rise—the doctors, lawyers, and engineers were back on their old income levels within six months after the mark was stabilized. The professionals who now flock to executive management programs and to refresher courses in engineering, accounting, law, and medicine may, in the end, turn out to be the only ones who are most nearly inflation-proof.

(1981)

CHAPTER TWO

A Scorecard for Management

"MANAGEMENT AUDITS" ARE HOTLY debated these days by business' friends and by its critics, by regulatory agencies, in management seminars, and in management journals. The proponents usually argue for a searching inquiry into basic management qualities—a management's morale and integrity, its creativity, its "social values," its human empathy, and so on. "Nonsense," snort the opponents. "The only thing that counts is performance, and that is measured by the bottom line."

Both sides, it can be said unequivocally, are wrong. There is a need to appraise management. Indeed, it is quite likely that boards of directors within a fairly short time will have imposed on them a legal duty to appraise the management of publicly held companies. But it is equally true that only performance can be appraised. The things which a proponent of management audits talks about—integrity or creativity, for instance—are better left to a novelist.

Yet the "bottom line" is not even an appropriate measure of management performance. The bottom line measures business performance rather than management performance. And the performance of a business today is largely a result of the performance, or lack of it, of earlier managements in years past.

Today's executives are, of course, a good deal more than passive custodians of the past. They can, and properly should, modify the decisions they inherit. Indeed to bail out these decisions when they go wrong, as all decisions in respect to the future are likely to do, is one of their most important and most difficult assignments. But today's executives are also charged with the responsibility for making the future of the business—with lead times that are becoming increasingly longer and in some areas range up to ten years or so.

Performance of management, therefore, means in large measure doing a good job in preparing today's business for the future. And this is an area in which measurement of management performance—or at least an appraisal of it—is needed the most.

Certainty regarding the performance of today's management is possible only by hindsight, that is, in the future. But appraisal with a high probability is possible today. For the future of a business is largely made by management performance in four areas, in each of which the batting average of a management can be ascertained, and in each of which a management can work on improving its performance once it knows its past record of hits and misses.

1. Performance in Appropriating Capital

Almost every company has elaborate procedures for capital appropriations. Even in companies in which divisional managers have almost complete freedom, top management keeps a tight rein on capital appropriations and reserves for itself the final decision on even fairly small capital investments. And most managements spend an enormous amount of time on capital appropriations decisions. But amazingly few managements pay much attention to what happens after the capital investment has been approved. In many companies there is no way even of finding out. To be sure, if the new multimillion-dollar plant falls behind schedule or costs a great deal more than was originally planned, everybody knows about it. But once a plant is "on stream," there is not too much attention paid to comparing its performance with the expectations that led to the investment. And smaller investments, though in their totality equally important, are barely ever looked at once the decision has been made.

Yet there are few better tests of the competence and performance of a management than its performance in appropriating capital, that is, the actual experience of capital investments measured against expectations. General Motors has known this for about sixty years; indeed, its system for monitoring the performance of managerial capital investment decisions was first published in 1927.

Since then we have known that we need to measure both return on the investment itself against the return expected when the investment decision was made and the impact of the investment decision on the return and profitability of the entire business, again against the expectations at the time the decision was made. To organize this feedback from the results of capital appropriation decisions is a fairly simple matter. It does not, except in the biggest and most complex companies, require a computer run but can be done on an ordinary spread sheet, kept in the bottom drawer. What is needed, however, is a willingness to commit oneself to expectations when the decision is being made and then the intellectual honesty to face up to the actual results rather than try not to have to look at them.

2. Performance on People Decisions

Everyone agrees that the development and placement of managerial and other professional people is the ultimate control of any organization. Indeed, it is the only way to make sure that today's decisions will bear fruit. By their very nature, decisions made with respect to the future—that is, managerial decisions which commit today's economic resources to future uncertainty—will run into serious difficulty. And then it all depends on the ability of tomorrow's people to bail out today's managerial decisions. Yet, while admitted to be crucial, the area is usually considered to be intangible. But neither what is expected of a person's performance when he is put into a job nor how the appointment works out is intangible. Perhaps they can't be quantified, but surely they can be judged—and fairly easily.

One thing we can be sure of when an appointment does not turn out as well as expected is that the executive who made the decision and who selected and appointed the person made the wrong decision or—equally often—made the decision the wrong way. To blame the failed promotion on the promoted person—as is usually done—is no more rational than to blame a capital investment that has gone sour on the money that was put in. Indeed, executives who know how one makes people decisions and who work on them do not accept the much-invoked "Peter Principle" in respect to their appointees. Few, very few, of the men they pick for promotions turn out to be incompetent. They never believe that good people decisions are made by "good judges of people." They know that they are made by executives who don't know how to judge people but who work hard on making people decisions, and especially by executives who make sure that they check how their people decisions actually work out in practice.

It is indeed not possible—or at least not easily possible—to judge, let alone to test, the spirit of an organization and the development of the people in it. But it is quite easy to test the results of spirit and development—that is the performance of decisions on people compared to the expectations underlying them.

3. Innovation Performance

What is expected from a research effort, from a development effort, from a new business or a new product? And what then are the actual results—one year, two years, three years, five years later? Research results cannot be predicted or projected forward, we are being told all the time. But surely the research results can be measured, or at least appraised, and can then be projected backward to the promises and expectations at the time the research effort was started. The same thing is equally true in respect to development efforts, to a new business, to a new product, to a new market, and to innovation.

Even the most competent management probably bats, at best, around 0.300 in the innovation area. Innovation is chancy. But surely there is a reason, other than luck, why some managements, a Procter & Gamble or a 3-M, for instance, have done consistently so much better in product development and product introduction than most others. One reason is that all the businesses with a high batting average systematically appraise their innovation performance against expectations. Then one can improve. And then, above all, one can know what one is good at. Most businesses manage innovation by promise. The competent innovators manage by results.

4. Planning Performance

Finally, the performance of management can and should be measured in respect to its business planning. Again, the question is what the results are compared to the expectations. Did the things predicted in the plan happen? And were they the truly important things? Were the goals set the right goals, in light of actual development, both within the business and in the market, economy, and society? And have they been attained?

Planning, it cannot be said too often, is not an attempt to predict the future, let alone an attempt to control it. It is an attempt to make today's decisions in contemplation of their futurity. Planning, therefore, whether done systematically or haphazardly, assumes expectations regarding the future. And whether these expectations are then borne out by actual events or contradicted by them is an acid test of management's performance. Again, this requires that expectations be defined, spelled out—and that there be organized feedback from actual events on the expectations. As in the innovation area, the most capable firm does not have a particularly high batting average in its business planning, something less than 0.300 I would assume. But, to continue the baseball metaphor, these managements at least know when they strike out or make a hit and above all they know what they do well and what they need to improve on.

Because planning, no matter how organized, is the process that commits the resources of a business to the future, planning performance is crucial to the performance of management's responsibility for making the future. Appraisal of planning performance, therefore, constitutes the last, though perhaps not the least, measurement of management's performance.

Even the greatest skill in these four areas is unlikely to help much if the company is in the wrong business. It is unlikely to make a profitable business out of the proverbial buggy-whip manufacturer or a growth company out of an old business in a mature industry— say a bread bakery. But at least skill and performance in these areas will show soon that a company is in yesterday's business or that it does not possess the economic characteristics that allow it to grow.

On the other hand, being in the right business and having the right objectives will not bring about performance unless management performs well—or at least adequately—in respect to capital investment decisions, people decisions, innovation, and planning. These four decision areas are not the essence of business management, but they are its test. And every management should subject itself to these tests.

(1976)

CHAPTER THREE

Helping Small Businesses Cope

BUSINESS GROWTH IS A REWARD for achievement and should be cause for joy. Instead, for far too many small- and medium-sized businesses, growth turns into nightmare. Just as the company seems poised for rapid and profitable growth, it gets out of control and into severe trouble.

Even if the business survives the crisis—and many do not—it often will have lost its earlier growth potential and remain permanently stunted. And in the most favorable case, the business that then recovers and goes on to success, there will be deep and permanent scars.

I have learned to apply five simple rules to enable a small- or medium-sized business to grow without getting out of control and without suffering the severe affliction of the growth crisis.

1.

Growth requires investment. It always strains the financial resources of a business. And unless the business is managed for cash flow, growth is likely to create liquidity pressures that might even force the growing business into insolvency. Profits in such a business come second. Indeed, in a rapidly growing business profits are an accounting delusion; they should be considered contingency reserves.

2.

The growing business, especially the growing small- or medium-sized business, needs to anticipate the financial structure and financial resources it will need—at least two and, better still, three years ahead. It needs to go to work now on obtaining the outside money it will need to sustain its growth.

Financial requirements of a business do not grow proportionately with sales volume. Some areas may need disproportionately more money, others disproportionately less. Receivables, for instance, may have to grow twice as fast as sales—but they may also grow only half as fast or hardly at all while sales double. And this applies in all areas—manufacturing plant and equipment; distributive facilities, such as warehouses or delivery fleets; investment in technical service or in materials inventories.

As a result, capital structure always needs to be changed during rapid growth. Today's structure always becomes inappropriate and a straitjacket. If tomorrow's financial needs and financial structure are tackled today—that is, a few years ahead of the need—a sound business can almost always obtain what it needs in the right amount and in the right form, whether equity, long-term debt, medium-term notes, or short-term commercial credit.

If the business waits until it needs the new money, it will have waited too long. Even if it can get what it needs, it is unlikely to be in the right form and almost certain to be very expensive.

Financial planning for the growing business need not be elaborate; indeed, it rarely can be elaborate. But it needs to be timely, and that means way ahead of the actual need. The starting point has to be the realization that growth is qualitative and changes financial needs and financial structure. Growth is not just "more"; it creates something new and different.

3.

To grow without running into the growth crisis, a business also needs to anticipate future information needs. Growth always requires data beyond those furnished by the accounting system—data on what goes on outside the business and especially data on what goes on in the marketplace.

I remember vividly a small company in the consumer goods business with a very successful innovative product range and a growth rate in sales of 10 to 15 percent compounded each year. The company announced a fairly sharp price increase but offered to supply present distributors with goods at the old prices for the rest of the year. Sales spurted by 50 percent that year. But after the first of the next year, sales completely dried up. Six months later, they had recovered to only half the earlier level. The company collapsed and was forced to liquidate.

Actually, nothing had happened except a lack of data. The ultimate consumer continued to increase his purchases at a 10 to 15 percent rate. But the distributors had stocked up in anticipation of the announced price increases and were holding back new orders until they had worked off their inventories.

Nobody in the company realized this, however, for everybody (mis)defined "sales" as deliveries to the distributors—the legal and accounting rather than the economic definition (and usually the wrong definition, by the way). The simplest sample of customer purchases—for instance, a sample of the actual sales by 1 percent of the distributors once a month—would have told the company early what was happening and would have enabled it to take the appropriate measures.

But lack of such simple data, as anyone familiar with small and growing businesses knows, is all too common. The small- and medium-sized business that expects to grow therefore needs to ask, "What additional information do we need to have real control and to know what really goes on in our business? What are real results in the business and what are real costs?" And it needs to develop this information well before the time at which its absence can cripple it.

4.

Small- and medium-sized businesses that want to grow need to concentrate on technologies, products, and markets. They need to free themselves by sloughing off diversions.

There is, for instance, the manufacturer who sells $12 million a year in his home market, the United States—up from $3 million five years ago—and who indulges himself in an international business, consisting of a joint venture in Japan and two small plants in Europe. After five years of hard work, they sell a total of $1.5 million and lose every year $600,000. Worse, they absorb up to one third of the time of all the key people in the company, who forever dash off to Osaka or Hamburg to "straighten things out"—without, however, ever staying long enough to achieve anything.

Or there is "our prestige line," the "flagship of our fleet," or— conversely—the "popular low-priced line" developed in an abortive attempt to get the company's goods to the discount stores and "to make us a factor in the mass market."

Growth makes large demands on energy, especially on managerial energy. It demands concentration on areas where the results are. And it demands willingness to give up areas in which there are only efforts but no real results, no matter how promising these areas looked when the company first went into them.

5.

The small- or medium-sized business usually cannot afford much by way of top management. But if it wants to grow, it better make sure that well ahead of time it develops the top management it will need when it has grown. Small, growth businesses start out typically as the brainchild of one or two men. These are usually entrepreneurs with vision, drive, ability, and courage. But they are still only human beings, and thus endowed with weaknesses as well as strengths.

There is the company, for instance, started by a man with high product imagination, great capacity for product design and development, and ability in promotion. He builds a fast-growing, highly successful small company on his ability. But this kind of man is often bereft of financial sense and tends to be a "loner," moody, and ill at ease with people.

If he is conscientious, he will almost certainly kill the business. He will force himself to work on finance and other tasks for which he lacks ability. By spending so much time on what he cannot do well he will neglect what he can do well. A few years later the growth crisis hits and this kind of company usually goes out of existence, having lost the original advantages its founder gave it.

Equally common is the man who brushes aside as unimportant any concern about people, finance, or distribution while he concentrates on product design, development, and promotion. Three or four years later his business will also be in crisis. Still, it can often be salvaged; at least it has the right products and they are positioned right in the marketplace. However, it is still likely to remain permanently stunted, while the owner-entrepreneur will probably lose control and be jettisoned in the course of the rescue operation.

What the small- and medium-sized business needs in order to grow is to ask: "What are the key activities in this business (and people and money are always key activities in every business, although never the only ones)?" Then its top people must ask: "Which key activities fit the people at the top?" Then: "Which of our associates have the capacity to take on, in addition to their current duties, the key activities for which the present managers are not suited?"

These people are then assigned responsibility for specific key activities, preferably without publicity, without change of title, and without being paid a penny more. Five years later, when the business has grown, it should then have the top management team it will need. But it takes five years or so to develop such a team, and if the job is not started beforehand the company will not be able to become or remain larger. It will buckle under the additional load that growth always imposes.

It is difficult if not impossible to cure the growth crisis of the small- or medium-sized business. But it is fairly easy to prevent such a crisis, and vital to do so.

(1977)

CHAPTER FOUR

Is Executive Pay Excessive?

MEASURED IN CONSTANT AFTER-TAX DOLLARS, incomes of corporation executives in the United States have been going down fairly steadily for the last thirty years. And the gap between the after-tax real income of top management people and of all other employees, from rank and file up through middle management, has been shrinking rather than widening during the same period.

Yet almost no one knows the facts, and almost no one believes them. What is widely believed is that executive compensation has been going up so fast as to have become "excessive," and that the inequality of incomes in U.S. corporations and in the U.S. economy is steadily increasing rather than decreasing.

One reason for this widespread impression is inflation and the impact it has on incomes under our progressive tax system. As money incomes rise, even though real incomes remain constant or go down, income tax rates go up.

A rank-and-file worker in American industry in 1977 made twice the money income he had made ten years ago, and with fringes his wage cost to his employer was at least two and a half times what it had been ten years earlier. But his taxes had at least tripled, especially as state and local taxes in many places had been added on top of federal taxes. This ratchet action, however, did not affect the top income earners—the people with earned income of $100,000 per family or more. Their federal tax take is limited to 50 percent of their earned income.

The second reason why executive compensation is widely considered excessive is the widespread use of tax gimmicks. To shield executives from the rapacity of the tax collector, corporations have availed themselves of every tax shelter or tax loophole that the law and lawyers have created.

Stock options are just one example. Most executives know that the explanations given for these gimmicks are pure hokum. I have yet to meet an executive who really believes that stock options act as an incentive or promote performance. Everyone knows that they are tax avoidance, pure and simple. Indeed, I have sat in on discussions between a company and an executive it wanted to hire which concerned *only* the net (after tax) sum which the executive was to receive and then turned the design of the right "package" over to the tax lawyers.

But it is hard to resist temptation. And so executive compensation plans have become festooned with tax gimmicks to the point where they have lost all shape and coherence.

The consequences have been far from wholesome. In a period of inflation, in particular, these tax gimmicks tend to impede responsible decisions. Even in the early years of inflation, in the early and mid-seventies, most companies knew that their published accounts misrepresented economic reality. They knew they showed inventory profits, for instance, that were pure inflation; or they showed profits that simply represented underdepreciation.

Yet whenever someone wanted to adjust accounts to economic reality he was stopped, lest this interfere with the value of the executives' stock options or with their profit-sharing bonus. "I would do it myself, of course," I have heard more than one chief executive officer say, "but I cannot do this to my colleagues."

Externally the effect has been much worse. These things create—and with good reason—the impression that executives are greedy, that they are out to fatten themselves at the expense of the business and that they are "ripping off" stockholders, employees, and customers alike.

At the same time, the tax gimmicks do not work. In the few companies I know which resisted the temptation to subordinate economic rationality to tax avoidance in structuring executive compensation—the few companies which just pay current cash or deferred cash and nothing else—executives have fared no worse than in companies that made the tax lawyers rich.

Oh yes, stock options worked beautifully during the bull market. But over a ten-year period, from 1966 to 1976, for instance, executives who did not have options, or phantom stock, or any of the other complicated tax-avoidance gimmicks have probably done as well as executives under plans that most skillfully took advantage of every single tax loophole a benevolent government offered.

Finally, but perhaps most important, very few top executives in very few, very big companies have truly enormous earnings. A few (*1981 note:* no more than thirty perhaps) have a total "compensation package" that comes to a million dollars or so, pre-tax. A larger number, although probably still no more than a thousand, have compensation packages with a total annual pre-tax value of $500,000 or more—including salary, bonus, stock options, retirement guarantees, severance pay, and so on.

Economically, these few very large executive salaries are quite unimportant. Socially, they do enormous damage. They are highly visible and highly publicized. And they are therefore taken as typical rather than as the extreme exceptions they are.

These few very large salaries are being explained by the "need" to pay "the market price" for executives. But this is nonsense. Every executive knows perfectly well that it is the internal logic of a hierarchical structure that explains them. The foreman has to get $15,000 after fringes or $20,000 including fringes. And each level above the foreman has to get at least 40 percent more it is believed. If there are thirty levels, then the top man has to get $500,000 plus, not because this is his "market value," but because otherwise the foreman could not be paid his $15,000.

Money is a status symbol which defines an executive's place in the corporate hierarchy. And the more levels there are, the more pay the man at the top has to get.

This rewards people for creating additional layers of management. I have seen it happen more than once: A division general manager jacks up his own base pay by 50 percent through "reorganizing" his division and creating five levels of management where there were three before.

Yet levels of management should be kept to the minimum. An executive plan that rewards executives for adding on levels is a threat to the health of the organization itself. If very large salaries can be justified only because the logic of hierarchical levels demands them, then perhaps the number of levels needs to be reduced. At the very least, there should be no reward for building levels—and the very large salaries are exactly that.

What needs to be done is fairly obvious. Business needs to take the initiative in eliminating, or at least in assuaging, the tax ratcheting of lower- and middle-income earners in an inflationary era. The most meaningful "tax reform," and incidentally the one on which unions would support business, is to adjust income tax rates to the rate of inflation. If this is not done, and soon, the 50 percent ceiling on the tax on earned income—that is the ceiling on tax on executive incomes—is almost bound to be done away with.

Executives thus have a direct self-interest in removing the tax penalty on lower and middle incomes. And such a reform would also be an effective way to restrain inflation by removing the incentive to government to raise revenues automatically by inflating the currency.

Finally, the most radical, but also the most necessary, innovation would be a published corporate policy that fixes the maximum compensation of all corporate executives, after all taxes but including all fringes, as a multiple of the after-tax income of the lowest paid regular full-time employee (including fringes).

The exact ratio is less important than that there should be such a ratio. For a small business it might be 15-to-1, which would mean an after-tax compensation package of $150,000 to $180,000 or around $300,000 pre-tax—which is far more than small- or medium-sized companies pay as a rule. For the large company a $250,000 to $300,000 top net, after-tax compensation package—i.e., a $400,000 to $450,000 pre-tax value—would represent a 25-to-1 ratio—and that would take care of all but a very small number of very large companies.

But even a 30-to-1 ratio—equal today (i.e., 1977) to $600,000 or so in pre-tax compensation including all fringes—would still be well below what employees, union leaders, college professors, newspaper reporters, and middle managers today think the ratio is. Most people put it at 50-to-1, or even at 100-to-1. A ratio of 25-to-1 is not equality. But it is well within the range most people in this country, including the great majority of rank-and-file workers, consider proper and indeed desirable.

There should, indeed there must, be exceptions. A "star," whether the supersalesman in the insurance company or the scientist in the lab who comes up with half a dozen highly profitable research breakthroughs, should be paid without any income limitation.

There should also, I am convinced, be a big extra award available for anyone, regardless of rank and title, who makes a truly extraordinary contribution well beyond "the call of duty." Every organization needs the equivalent of the Congressional Medal of Honor or of the Victoria Cross.

If and when the attack on the "excessive compensation of executives" is launched—and I very much fear that it will come soon— business will complain about the public's "economic illiteracy" and will bemoan the public's "hostility to business." But business will have only itself to blame. It is a business responsibility, but also a business self-interest, to develop a sensible executive compensation structure that portrays economic reality and asserts and codifies the achievement of U.S. business in this century: the steady narrowing of the income gap between the "big boss" and the "working man."

(1977)

CHAPTER FIVE

On Mandatory Executive Retirement

THE MOST INTELLIGENT PROVISION—and the most needed one—in the recent (i.e., 1978) law extending the mandatory retirement age for private-sector employees to seventy (and eliminating it altogether for government employees) is the provision which permits the mandatory retirement of senior executives at age sixty-five.

Unless the seniors vacate top-executive slots, the juniors cannot move up. And in the next ten years, as the babies of the "baby boom" reach middle age, there will be a press of young and ambitious executives between thirty and forty hungry for promotion and well qualified for it. Also, the one affliction of which the sufferer himself is totally unaware is senility; and senility in high places is one of the most dangerous degenerative diseases of an organization.

Yet as the law is written and commonly interpreted, it will not be enforceable and will not be enforced—nor is it desirable that it be. What is both enforceable and desirable is a policy—and it is well within the law as it stands—under which senior executives are forced to step down at age sixty-five but may continue until the new normal retirement age of seventy in a nonexecutive capacity. That's now the law in our largest state, California, under a retirement bill passed in 1977.

But in the rest of the country we will soon find that to retire senior executives at sixty-five when all the others can stay on until seventy simply won't work. How many people in the labor force will want to stay on and keep working full-time past age sixty-five we do not know as yet. But we do know that the desire to retire diminishes sharply the higher up a man climbs on the occupational and career ladders.

Coal miners are perfectly happy, as a rule, to retire well before sixty-five after a lifetime underground. Senior executives, almost without exception, dread retirement, as do doctors and lawyers. They have started later. Physically the work is not nearly as demanding as most blue-collar jobs. These men may talk of the joys of hunting and fishing, of golf, and of reading all the books they missed. But as a rule, they can barely stand a six-week vacation away from their work. For their work—unlike that of the coal miner's—interests them, indeed tends to absorb them.

And so compulsory retirement of senior executives at age sixty-five, while welcomed by everybody else, will be sabotaged by the senior executives themselves—if retirement means being driven out to pasture. If we insist on retirement at sixty-five when the other people are allowed, if not encouraged, to stay on, we will increasingly find that the ablest and most accomplished men of age fifty-five will refuse promotion to senior executive jobs requiring retirement at age sixty-five. We will then increasingly look to second-raters for the top jobs.

The senior executive at age sixty-five who is physically and mentally in good shape, as the majority are these days, is too valuable a resource to discard. The present retirement age of sixty-five was set in the mid-twenties in this country; biologically, a man of that age today is equivalent to a man of fifty-three back then. He's just at his peak.

Nonetheless, population pressures may make it necessary to free the job position he holds. The only sensible policy is one that provides for the senior man to leave the executive suite at age sixty-five but then continue working as an individual professional, provided, of course, that he wants to.

This may sound like a radical innovation. "Stepping down" is something people always think cannot be done—and "stepping down" in this case clearly entails getting less money and having much less power. But it is already standard practice in some companies and has caused no problems wherever introduced. At Westinghouse Electric, for instance, officers give up executive duties and titles at age sixty and become "counselors."

The retiring executive's pension would be based on his five years of highest pay during the last ten or twelve years, rather than on the last five years of full-time employment, in order to avoid a financial penalty for longer service.

The main thing to do is to work out with the executive the role which he should assume when he steps out of the vice presidency or presidency. This requires advance preparation, beginning, experience indicates, at least six months, but rarely more than one year, before the actual date. (Don't start too soon. People aren't ready to think about their "stepping down" until they have to.)

The man's future role requires careful thought on what might be called "career continuation" or "career extension." What is the individual really good at? What is he really interested in? But also: What are the most important needs of the company?

The vice president of marketing, for instance, may be the right man to take over a major product-development assignment or to work out, develop, test, and put in place a new policy for product introductions. Or he may be the best man to shepherd a clutch of small entrepreneurial businesses the large company has financed in partnership with individual owner-entrepreneurs. The sixty-five-year-old treasurer of the company's international division may be the ideal man to train the company's financial people throughout the world on foreign-exchange management and inflation accounting.

Some of these assignments may be full-time and last for years. Others start out full-time and taper off gradually. Others are part-time from the start. But all of them use the skills, experience, and status of a senior man where he can make a major contribution. Yet they move him out of executive and managerial responsibility, with its burdens, its time constraints, and its pressures.

The executive who wants a "second career"—and an increasing number of men in business do—had better start earlier. A man's mid-forties are the best time to think through what he wants out of life and to change careers. The pension is then usually vested and the kids are grown up; and by then people know what they are good at, what they can do, and what they like to do. Becoming a professional director—working full-time as a part-time member of four or five boards—would be one possibility. Seasoned directors are increasingly in demand.

But the majority of senior executives will want to stay in executive work as long as they can, that is until age sixty-five. And unless a person has changed careers earlier and knows how to do it, he is somewhat old for a second career at age sixty-five. But he is the right age for career continuation or career extension.

It shouldn't be difficult to work out what an executive could take on at age sixty-five. But often it will require an outsider, not necessarily a psychologist or personnel specialist, but someone who isn't part of the problem and can talk freely and in confidence with both the executive and the company. It will require someone who can tell the executive frankly that he will cease to be an executive; he will once again be one of the "working stiffs," unable to "whistle up" the company plane on demand or sit on the management committee or even the board of directors. His alternative, it should be made clear, is retirement.

All this may sound like "big-company stuff." And indeed so far only big companies, to the best of my knowledge, have concerned themselves with career extension of the executive at sixty-five. But the new retirement law that permits retirement at age sixty-five from the executive position for the senior man should make career extension even more of a concern for the small- and middle-sized business. There the need to attract and hold able young people is usually acute; and the need to free senior positions is thus particularly great. But there also the competence, the knowledge, the skills, and the dedication which the senior executive of sixty-five represents are often far more needed and far more difficult to replace than in the big business.

To withdraw from the burden of managing at the top at age sixty-five is sensible for individual and company alike—but only if we use it as an opportunity to put to work the individual's strengths and his proven performance capabilities, for his own sake but also for that of the business, of the society, and of the economy.

(1978)

CHAPTER SIX

The Real Duties of a Director

SINCE JUNE 1978 THE BOARD OF DIRECTORS of every company listed on the New York Stock Exchange has been required by Exchange rules to have an audit committee of independent directors. Only in a few companies, however, has a key question yet been sufficiently explored: What are the responsibilities of this committee, and how should it go about its job?

Indeed, the responsibilities and work of the board of directors as a whole is a subject that has received too little attention in most companies. Yet it is increasingly clear that this will be a central question and a major challenge to top management and directors alike. The regulatory agencies, such as the Securities and Exchange Commission, increasingly demand more responsibility from the board and proof that the board takes these responsibilities seriously. Increasingly the courts are holding boards and board members to very high and demanding standards of accountability in stockholder suits. The only way for a board to protect itself against what might otherwise be unbearable liabilities is to think through its responsibilities carefully and to organize itself for discharging them.

The law still calls the board the "managing organ" of the corporation. This nineteenth-century formulation has become totally untenable and is not taken seriously by anyone. What the boards are, and must be, is the organ that makes sure that the company is being managed, to paraphrase a recent California decision.

The first requirement, therefore, is that the board makes sure that the company has a top management competent to run the business. The first task of a functioning board is to insist that company management design adequate yardsticks of performance for itself. In most businesses such yardsticks are needed in four areas, in addition of course to the traditional return-on-investment yardstick. Top management needs to be judged by its performance in allocating capital, by its performance in appointing people to managerial and other key positions, by its performance in respect to innovation, and by the adequacy and reliability of strategic plans.

In each of these areas top management should be required by a functioning board to spell out its expectations and to be judged, a few years later, by results as measured against these expectations.

Equally important is the duty of directors to make sure that top management itself is properly structured and properly staffed. It is the duty of the board not to tolerate mediocrity in high places. Today most boards will act only if there is gross malfunction in top management—and this is not enough.

The board also needs to make sure that top management has thought through the succession to top management jobs. Directors are responsible for making sure that top management and the company are properly organized. And finally, the board needs to make sure that the company, especially the larger one, has an adequate program for developing future managers and for testing executives before putting them into responsible and decision-making positions.

It is the job of the board to make sure that top management think through what business the company is in and what business it should be in. But equally important—and very rarely paid any attention—is the question of what business or businesses a specific company should not be in, what it should abandon or play down, and what it should slough off to keep itself lean and muscular.

The board of directors cannot work out a company's strategy. This requires both full-time work and inside knowledge of a business, its markets, its products, its technologies. But it is the duty of a board to make sure that a company, and especially a large publicly owned one, has adequate strategies and that these strategies are tested against actual results.

A board, to live up to its responsibility to make sure the business is being managed, must demand of top management that it think through and set goals for the productivity of resources. This is, after all, the first duty of any management: to make resources productive is what management is being paid for. A board needs to demand that top management know the productivity of capital in its business and set specific goals to improve productivity wherever substantial amounts of money are being invested, whether this be plant and equipment or receivables. The company needs, similarly, goals for the productivity of people, for the productivity of key physical resources (such as shelf space in a retail business), and—most crucial of them all—for the productivity of time for such groups as salesmen, engineers, researchers, or service personnel, whose main resource is time.

Finally, the board is responsible for making sure that a company has adequate policies for its key outside relationships—with government, with labor unions, with the public in general—and that it has adequate policies with respect to its legal and regulatory responsibilities. And then a board has to demand that there are adequate performance standards in these areas against which a company's actual results can be measured.

There is one additional area which should probably be included among the responsibilities and the work assignments of a functioning board of directors—the pension fund. The pension fund is increasingly going to be the main recipient of a company's earnings. And pension liabilities are increasingly going to be the greatest liabilities of American businesses. The board will not, as a rule, be able or willing to manage the pension fund itself. But it needs to supervise the management of the fund, both in respect to the adequacy of pension-fund contributions and the performance of pension-fund management.

In addition, in every business there are specific matters which top management will bring to the board, or should bring to the board: decisions on an acquisition or on dropping a product line; decisions on any lawsuit brought against the company; decisions on long-range research programs. Any board will supervise operating results, the company's liquidity, and all the other matters which today occupy the time and attention of the board, practically to the exclusion of concern with the fundamentals of managing. But in the areas which determine whether a company is indeed being managed or whether it drifts—that is, in the areas mentioned above—a board needs increasingly to think through its own role. It needs increasingly to develop its own goals and objectives. And it needs to think through which individuals should be held accountable for achieving the board's objectives.

Today there is a great deal of discussion regarding the membership of the board of directors of the American corporation. Harold Williams, the chairman of the SEC in the Carter Administration and himself a former board member with broad experience, argues strongly for our switching to a board which is totally independent of management in its composition, with the chief executive officer the only member of management on the board. There is strong criticism of the tradition of putting people on the board who render services to the company, such as lawyers or underwriters. And there are many people who question the propriety of retired executives continuing to sit on the board of a company which they once served as full-time members of management. Equally, there is increasing debate as to whether the board needs its own staff. To whom, for instance, should a company's internal auditors report— to top management or the audit committee of the board? (The answer is, clearly, to both.)

And beyond the present debate there is going to be another major task: the board functioning as the company's representative for relationships with different publics and constituencies, whether racial minorities or women or consumers or employees.

But the first item on the agenda is not the membership of the board. Before we can intelligently discuss how to staff, we have to know what the work and the assignments are. The first item on the agenda, therefore, is the specific responsibilities of the directors and the work needed in order to discharge them.

(1978)

CHAPTER SEVEN

The Information Explosion

WHETHER AND WHEN THE "office of the future" will become reality, and what it will actually look like, are still largely conjecture. But the main impacts of the new mini-processor-based information technology are already predictable—and in some cases already with us.

The first impact will probably be a sharp drop in business travel. Few businessmen traveled before 1950 or so, and none, except salesmen, traveled a great deal. But as soon as the jet appeared, two decades ago, hopping a plane for a two-day meeting in Paris, Rio, or Tokyo became commonplace for senior executives and even more so for their immediate subordinates.

Whether this is the most effective way to get things done or get to know people is debatable. But the advantage of direct access, face to face, to associates, partners, and customers in faraway places so greatly outweighed the fatigue and cost of air travel as to encourage gross overindulgence in it.

Now increasingly there will be alternative ways to meet and "share a common experience." No matter how far from each other, executives will more and more be able to "meet in the same room," see each other eye to eye, talk to each other face to face, and exchange reports and graphs, all without physically leaving their own offices. Several satellites, now under construction and expected to begin operations within a few years, will transmit pictures, voices, and graphics simultaneously to earth stations that are linked with business subscribers—and thus be able to simulate the three-dimensional space of a real conference room in a subscriber's office.

Executives will therefore have to think more carefully about what to use physical travel for; truly to know another person, for example, will probably always require a real, rather than a simulated, presence. But at the same time executives will have to learn what very few of them know so far: how to prepare, organize, run, and follow up a short meeting for both achievement and mutual understanding.

For the last twenty-five years or so, management scientists and computer specialists have been talking a great deal about total information systems. Now the hardware is available. A good many managers, especially in large companies, already have on their desks a mini-processor, which combines a small computer for their own use with a terminal for the company's large computer system, complete with a small display screen and, frequently, with print-out for durable copy. Within a few years this will become standard equipment, like the telephone on the desk or the hand-held calculator—and the executive mini-processor may well be no larger than a telephone is today.

With the advent of the desk-top mini-processor, the manager risks being overloaded with paper and data. Indeed, the critical problem will not be how to get or how to process information, but rather to define what information really is. This is a task that cannot be left to that mythical creature, the "information specialist." Information is the manager's main tool, indeed the manager's "capital," and it is he who must decide what information he needs and how to use it.

Managers will also have to come to grips with some critical questions about the role of information in their organizations. Who shall have access to what information? How can information be protected against fraud, industrial espionage, or prying and gossip-mongering? How can personal privacy be guarded? How can confidential information be confined to those who are legitimately entitled to it, without a secretiveness which encourages scuttlebutt and demoralizes?

Over the last hundred years, armies have worked out useful rules to deal with these problems: A manager needs to know everything that pertains to his own work and to that of the level immediately above him. Information beyond this may be of interest to him, but has little relevance and should basically be restricted. Almost no one, outside of the military, has tried to convert this rule into policy so far; even the military still has a long way to go. Yet without such a policy the new information capacity can only endanger both performance and organization morale.

The greatest impact of the new information technology, however, will not be on the human organization but on the production process. Mini-processors are beginning to regulate the operation of machines and tools, a process that is already far advanced in numerically controlled machine tools, medical instruments, all kinds of testing equipment, and increasingly in aircraft and automobile engines.

This integration of information processing with productive machinery amounts to a third industrial revolution. The second one began roughly a century ago, when machines were first combined directly with fractional horsepower motors. Until then, power—whether produced by water, steam engine, or dynamo—had to be transmitted to machines by belts or pulleys, which in turn meant that power-driven equipment had to be very close to the source of power. A few hundred yards was the limit of distance.

The fractional horsepower motor made possible the central power station. It made possible the modern factory. It gave both flexibility and economy. By 1920 or so, the transmission belt had become obsolete and modern industrial production had emerged. Ten years later the fractional horsepower motor had taken over the oldest domestic appliance around, the sewing machine. And by 1950 it had been integrated with the typewriter, the toothbrush, and the carving knife. The fractional horsepower motor, in effect, took heavy manual work out of the productive process.

The third industrial revolution, in which information processing is becoming part of the machine or the tool, will shift production from being manual to being knowledge-based. Before the second industrial revolution there were journeymen and laborers. Afterward, the greatest expansion was in the number of semiskilled machinetenders and, more important, skilled workers. Within the next twenty years the center of gravity is likely to shift to technologists—people whose contributions are based more on formal schooling and theory than on apprenticeship and skill.

There is a good deal of talk today about the need to re-industrialize America, to restore the country's capacity to manufacture capital goods productively and competitively. To do this, however, will require a shift to the third industrial revolution—that is, to the integration of information processing and production in machines and tools.

Only such integration can make productive the one resource where this country and indeed all industrially developed countries have an advantage, namely, highly schooled people. From now on, in all developed countries, there will be an increasing shortage of young people available for traditional manual work, skilled or unskilled. Tremendously large populations in the developing countries will be available for traditional manual work, and will be willing, or forced, to work for very low wages, even as they rapidly improve their productivity. In such a world, only the integration of information processing and production can maintain and improve the standards of living for workers in the already developed countries.

The mini-processor will thus provide tremendous opportunities for the industrial economies. But it will also impose tremendous demands on businessmen and on the economy—demands on capital equipment, demands on substantial shifts in productive organization, and, above all, demands on the management of people at work.

(1980)

CHAPTER EIGHT

Learning from Foreign Management

WHAT CAN WE LEARN from American management? was the question asked all over the world only ten years ago. Now it is perhaps time to ask: What can American management learn from others in the free world, and especially from management in Western Europe and Japan? For Europe and Japan now have the managerial edge in many of the areas which we used to consider American strengths, if not American monopolies.

First, foreign managers increasingly demand responsibility from their employees, all the way down to the least skilled blue-collar worker on the factory floor. They are putting to work the tremendous improvement in the education and skill of the labor force that has been accomplished in this century. The Japanese are famous for their "quality circles" and their "continuous learning." Employees at all levels come together regularly, sometimes once a week, more often twice a month, to address the question: What can we do to improve what we already are doing? In Germany a highly skilled senior worker known as the *Meister* acts as teacher, assistant, and standard-setter rather than as supervisor and boss.

Second, foreign managers have thought through their benefits policies more carefully. Fringes in the United States are now as wide as in any other country, that is they amount to some forty cents for each dollar paid in cash wages. But in this country many benefits fail to benefit the individual employee. In many families, for instance, both husband and wife are docked the full family health-insurance premium at work, even though one insurance policy would be sufficient. And we pay full Social Security charges for the married working woman, even though married working women under our Social Security system may never see a penny of their money paid into their accounts.

By contrast, foreign managements, especially those of Japan and Germany, structure benefits according to the needs of recipients. The Japanese, for instance, set aside dowry money for young unmarried women, while they provide housing allowances to men in their early thirties with young families. In England a married woman in the labor force can opt out of a large part of old-age insurance if her husband already pays for the couple at his place of employment.

Third, foreign managers take marketing seriously. In most American companies marketing still means no more than systematic selling. Foreigners today have absorbed more fully the true meaning of marketing: knowing what is value for the customer.

American managers can learn from the way foreigners look at their products, technology, and strategies from the point of view of the market rather than vice versa. Foreigners are increasingly thinking in terms of market structure, trying to define specific market niches for their products, and designing their businesses with a marketing strategy in mind. The Japanese automobile companies are only one example. Few companies are as attentive to the market as the high-technology and high-fashion entrepreneurs of northern Italy.

It is not correct, as is so often asserted in this country, that Japanese and Western European businesses subordinate profits. Indeed, the return on total assets is conspicuously higher today in a great many foreign businesses than it is in this country, especially if profits are adjusted for inflation. But the foreign manager has increasingly learned to say, "It is my job to earn a proper profit on what the market wants to buy." We still, by and large, try to say in this country, "What is our product with the highest profit margin? Let's try to sell that, and sell it hard."

Incidentally, when the foreign manager says "market," he tends to think of the world economy. Very few Japanese companies actually depend heavily on exports. And yet it is the rare Japanese business which does not start out with the world economy in marketing, even if its own sales are predominantly in the Japanese home market.

Fourth, foreign managements base their marketing and innovation strategies on the systematic and purposeful abandonment of the old, the outworn, and the obsolete. In every single business plan of a major foreign company I have seen lately—Japanese, German, French, and so on—the first question is not "What are the new things we are going to do?" The first question is "What are the old things we are going to abandon?" As a result, resources are available for innovation, new products, new markets. In too many American companies, the most productive resources are frozen into defending yesterday.

Fifth, foreign managements keep separate and discrete those areas where short-term results are the proper measurement and those where results should be measured over longer time spans, such as innovation, product development, product introduction, and manager development. The quarterly P and L is taken as seriously in Tokyo and Osaka as it is in New York and Chicago; and, with the strong role that the banks play in the management of German companies, the quarterly P and L is probably taken more seriously in Frankfurt than it is in the United States. But outside the United States, the quarterly P and L is increasingly being confined to the 90 percent or so of the budget that is concerned with operations and with the short term.

There is then a second budget, usually no more than a few percent of the total, which deals with those areas in which expenditures have to be maintained over a long period of time to get any results. By separating short-term operating budgets from longer-term investment or opportunities budgets, foreign companies can plan for the long haul. They can control expenditures over the long term and get results for long-term efforts and investments.

Sixth, managers in large Japanese, German, and French companies see themselves as national assets and leaders responsible for the development of proper policies in the national interest. One good example may be a group that came to see me in January of 1980. The chief executive officers of the forty largest Japanese companies came to discuss how Japan should adjust to demographic changes; official retirement age is still fifty-five in Japan, while life expectancy is now closer to eighty.

"We don't want to discuss with you," said the leader of the group, "what we in Japanese business should be doing. Our agenda is what Japan should be doing and what the best policies are in the national interest. Only after we have thought through the right national policies, and have defined and publicized them, are we going to think about the implications for business and for our companies. Indeed, we should postpone discussing economics altogether until we have understood what the right social policies are and what is best for the individual Japanese and for the country as a whole. Who else besides the heads of Japan's large companies can really look at such a problem from all aspects? To whom else can the country really look for guidance and leadership in such a tremendous change as that of the age structure of our population?"

Any American executive, at all conversant with our management literature, will now say, "What else is new? Every one of these things I have known for thirty years or so." But this is precisely the point. What we can learn from foreign management is not what to do. What we can learn is to do it.

Each of these six practices is American in origin. Every one the foreigners have learned from us in the thirty years they have come to this country to find out how to manage.

The "quality circles" for productivity and quality improvement which are now being touted in American industry as the latest and most advanced "innovation" were brought to Japan in the fifties and sixties by three Americans—Edwards Deming and Joseph M. Juran, both then at New York University, and A. V. Feigenbaum of General Electric.

The German *Meister* has ancient roots, but its present form dates back to the fifties and to unashamed imitation of the way IBM, first in this country and then in its European subsidiaries, had restructured the role and job of the first-line supervisor, converting him or her from a foreman into an assistant and teacher.

The Japanese and Germans practice in marketing what every American marketing textbook has been preaching for the last thirty years. The distinction between short-term and long-term budget goes back to DuPont and General Motors in the twenties. Indeed, each of these practices can be found in any management book written in the late forties and early fifties, including mine. We don't need to learn what the rules are—we invented them. What we need is to put them into practice.

(**1980**)

PART II

Business Performance

What is the measurement of performance in a business? The bottom line is the standard answer. But how does one truly measure the bottom line? Everyone talks of profit—for some it is the executive's Holy Grail, for others it is a dirty word. But what is profit really? How does any business, its executives, its investors, its employees, know whether a company's reported profit is good or inadequate? Actually, the record profits trumpeted by many companies' managements fall far short of covering genuine and identifiable costs, inflation, the costs of staying in business, costs which while not payable until tomorrow have already been incurred.

This section deals with performance within a business. But much of it applies equally to nonbusiness and not-for-profit institutions. For they, too, exist to perform.

CHAPTER NINE

The Delusion of Profits

BUSINESSMEN HABITUALLY COMPLAIN about the economic illiteracy of the public, and with good reason. The greatest threat to the free enterprise system in this country is not the hostility to business of a small, strident group, but the pervasive ignorance throughout our society in respect to both the structure of the system and its functioning.

But the same businessmen who so loudly complain about economic illiteracy are themselves the worst offenders. They don't seem to know the first thing about profit and profitability. And what they say to each other as well as to the public inhibits both business action and public understanding.

For the essential fact about profit is that there is no such thing. There are only costs.

What is called "profit" and reported as such in company accounts is genuine and largely quantifiable cost in three respects: as a genuine cost of a major resource, namely capital; as a necessary insurance premium for the real—and again largely quantifiable—risks and uncertainties of all economic activity; and as cost of the jobs and pensions of tomorrow. The only exception, the only true surplus, is a genuine monopoly profit such as that now being extorted by the OPEC cartel in petroleum.

1.

All economists have known for two hundred years that there are factors of production, that is, three necessary resources: labor, land (i.e., physical resources), and capital. And all of us should have learned in the last ten years that there are no "free" resources. They all have a cost. Indeed, the economists are way ahead of most businessmen in their understanding and acceptance of a genuine "cost of capital." Some of them, such as Ezra Solomon, a former member of the Council of Economic Advisers now back at Stanford University, have worked out elegant methods both for determining the cost of capital and for measuring the performance of a business in earning it.

We know that in the post-World War II period, until the onset of global inflation in the mid-sixties, the cost of capital in all developed countries of the Free World ran somewhat above 10 percent a year (it is almost certainly much higher in Communist economies). And we know that very few businesses actually earn enough to cover these genuine costs. But so far only a handful of businesses seem to know that there is such a cost. Fewer still seem to know whether they cover it or not. And even these few never talk about it and never in their published accounts subject their own performance to the test. Yet not to earn the cost of capital is as much a failure to cover costs as not to earn the costs of wages or of raw materials.

2.

Economic activity is the commitment of existing resources to future expectations. It is a commitment, therefore, to risk and uncertainty—in respect to obsolescence of products, processes, and equipment; in respect to changes in markets, distributive channels, and consumer values; and in respect to changes in economy, technology, and society. The odds in any commitment to the future are always adverse; it is not given to human beings to know the future. The odds, therefore, are always in favor of loss rather than gain. And in a period of rapid change such as ours, the risks and uncertainties are surely not getting smaller.

These risks and uncertainties are not capable of precise determination. But the *minimum* of risk in these commitments to the future is capable of being determined, and indeed quantified, with a fair degree of probability. Where this has been attempted in any business—and in both Xerox and IBM, for instance, it is known to have been done for years in respect to products and technologies—the risks have proven to be much higher than even conservative "business plans" assumed.

The risks of natural events—fire, for instance—have long been treated as normal business costs. A business that failed to set aside the appropriate insurance premiums for such risks would rightly be considered to be endangering the wealth-producing assets in its keeping. Economic, technological, and social risks and uncertainties are no less real. They too require an adequate "insurance premium"— and to supply it is the function of profit and profitability.

Therefore, the proper question for any management is not "What is the *maximum* profit this business can yield?" It is "What is the *minimum* profitability needed to cover the future risks of this business?" And if the profitability falls short of this minimum—as it does in most companies I know—the business fails to cover genuine costs, endangers itself, and impoverishes the economy.

3.

Profit is also tomorrow's jobs and tomorrow's pensions. Both are costs of a business and, equally, costs of the economy. Profit is not the only source of capital formation; there is also private savings, of course. But business earnings, whether retained in the business or paid out (returned to the capital market), are the largest single source of capital formation for tomorrow's jobs and, at least in the United States, the largest single source of capital formation for tomorrow's pensions.

The most satisfactory definition of "economic progress" is a steady rise in the ability of an economy to invest more capital for each new job and thereby to produce jobs that yield a better living as well as a better quality of work and life. By 1965, before inflation made meaningful figures increasingly difficult to obtain, investment per job in the American economy had risen from $35,000 to $50,000. The requirement will go up fairly sharply, for the greatest investment needs and opportunities are in industries: energy, the environment, transportation, health care, and, above all, increased food production, in which capital investment per job is far higher than the average in the consumer goods industries, which have dominated the economy these last twenty-five years.

At the same time, the number of jobs required is going up sharply—the aftermath of the "baby boom" between 1948 and 1960. We will have to increase the number of people at work by 1 percent, or almost a million people, each year until the early eighties to stay even with the demographics. At the same time, the number of people on pensions will also increase, if only because workers reaching retirement age will live longer, and so will the income expectations of the pensioners. Any company which does not produce enough capital, i.e., enough earnings, to provide for this expansion in jobs and pensions fails both to cover its own predictable and quantifiable costs and the costs of the economy.

These three kinds of costs—the costs of capital, the risk premium of economic activity, and the capital needs of the future—overlap to a considerable extent. But any company should be expected to cover adequately the largest of these three costs. Otherwise it operates at a genuine, certain, and provable loss.

There are three conclusions from these elementary premises:

1. Profit is not peculiar to capitalism. It is a prerequisite for any economic system. Indeed, the Communist economies require a much higher rate of profit. Their costs of capital are higher. And central planning adds an additional and major economic uncertainty. In fact, the Communist economies do operate at a substantially higher rate of profit than any market economy, no matter that for ideological reasons it is called "turnover tax" rather than "profit." And the only economies that can be considered as being based on profit planning are precisely Communist economies in which the producer (state planner) imposes the needed profitability in advance rather than let market forces determine it.

2. The costs which are paid for out of the difference between current revenues and current expenses of production and distribution are fully as much economic reality as wages or payments for supplies. Since a company's accounts are supposed to reflect economic reality, these costs should be shown. They are, to be sure, not as precisely known or knowable as the accountants' "costs of doing business" supposedly are. But they are known and knowable within limits that are probably no wider or fuzzier than those of most cost accounting or depreciation figures—and they may be more important both for managing a business and for analyzing its performance. Indeed, it might not be a bad idea to tie executive bonuses and incentives to a company's performance in earning adequately these genuine costs rather than to profit figures that often reflect financial leverage as much as actual economic performance.

3. Finally, businessmen owe it to themselves and owe it to society to hammer home that there is no such thing as profit. There are only costs: costs of doing business and costs of staying in business; costs of labor and raw materials, and costs of capital;

costs of today's jobs, and costs of tomorrow's jobs and tomorrow's pensions.

There is no conflict between profit and social responsibility. To earn enough to cover the genuine costs, which only the so-called profit can cover, is economic and social responsibility—indeed it is the specific social and economic responsibility of business. It is not the business that earns a profit adequate to its genuine costs of capital, to the risks of tomorrow and to the needs of tomorrow's worker and pensioner, that "rips off" society. It is the business that fails to do so.

(1975)

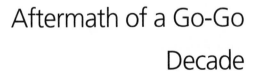

Aftermath of a Go-Go Decade

EVERY FIFTY OR SIXTY YEARS, these past 250 years, there has been a decade in which businessmen, politicians, and economists in the world economy's developed countries expected speculative growth to go on forever at an exponential rate: between 1710 and 1720; around 1770; after 1830; around 1870; and around 1910 (aborted in Europe by World War I but continuing in the United States until 1929); and finally the 1960s.

Every such era believed that there would be no limit to growth. And every one ended in debacle and left behind a massive hangover.

After every go-go decade prophecies of zero growth become popular. But except for the years between World War I and World War II, vigorous economic growth always either continued or was resumed very soon after the go-go years had come to an end. However, the aftermath of a speculative era always does bring substantial structural changes in the economy. Economic growth always changes and shifts to new foundations. And the demands on business management always change so greatly that what was considered smart management during the time of rapid expansion fast becomes inappropriate … if not stupid.

Some of the changes that the aftermath of the fast-action sixties is bringing about can be seen clearly.

1.

The balance sheet is again becoming as important as the P and L and may become more important. Liquidity and cash flow are replacing price-earnings ratios as managerial lodestars. Return on total assets is likely to become a more popular—as it surely is a more meaningful—yardstick than earnings per share.

Capital investment rather than consumption will have to become the engine of economic growth in the years ahead. The worldwide boom from the end of World War II until 1970 was largely fueled by consumer demand. From now on, the center of economic growth will be in areas which require large and massive capital investments: energy, the environment, transportation, and increased food production.

Above all, the great need of the next decade will be jobs, which require capital investment on a very large and steadily rising scale. In the United States we will, each year into the eighties, have to find some 30 percent to 50 percent more jobs for young entrants into the labor force than we needed in any year during the fifties and sixties. It will not be until the eighties that the "baby bust" that began in 1960–61 will have an impact on the number of new job-seekers, that the pressure of labor-force growth will lessen sharply.

In the developing countries the need for capital to create new jobs will be even greater. The babies of the late fifties and sixties who— unlike the babies of earlier generations—did not die in infancy, have grown to adulthood, and are streaming into the labor force.

At the same time, capital market structure is changing. The main channels for capital supply in this country are by now private pension funds. Even without inflation (and inflation has arrived with a vengeance), they will have to expand to satisfy the require-ments of the Employee Retirement Income Security Act (ERISA) of 1974. We are thus in the process of switching capital formation from entrepreneurs, whose job it is to invest in the future, to trust-ees, whose duty has always been to invest in prudent investments, which usually means the past.

A growing share of the national income in every developed country goes into governmental transfer payments, which convert potential savings into consumption. And government deficits have the same effect. Unless there is a severe and prolonged depression, capital will, therefore, predictably, be in short supply—at least through the rest of this decade and probably well into the eighties.

With the passing of the go-go years the relationship between interest rate differentials and liquidity preferences has changed sharply, and with it the rules for borrowing and investment. During the sixties, interest rate differentials were high. Short-term bank loans were cheap for most of this period. Even the apparently very high interest charges of the last few years actually represented zero interest rates, if adjusted for inflation. Long-term borrowing was, by contrast, quite expensive. And cost of equity capital was to become astronomical for all but the stock market darlings of the moment.

During this period of abundant bank money, a short-term, open bank loan was almost as dependable a source of funds for a reason-ably solvent borrower as long-term debt, and much cheaper. It was, therefore, rational behavior on the part of management—or at least it seemed so—to finance one's business as much as possible with short-term and cheap open bank loans, while at the same time trying to boost price-earnings ratios in the stock market to attain acclaim as a growth stock.

During any go-go decade managers tend to believe that "maxi-mizing earnings per share" is the same thing as "maximizing profit." They tend to forget completely that "maximizing profit" is not an end in itself, but a means toward minimizing the cost of the capital a business needs.

In the period ahead "maximizing earnings per share" may become largely inappropriate. Maximizing total return on all assets should become increasingly the right way, with considerable consequences for financial structure. Leverage—as fashionable these last ten or fifteen years as in any earlier go-go period—then becomes dubious, if not outright wrong. [*1981 note:* If the stock market signals anything, it is this change. On every one of the world's major stock exchanges most prices since the mid-seventies have not reflected earnings per share. They tend to reflect liquidity, cash flow, and defensive strength—that is, return on assets.]

If there is need for a shift from profit planning to asset management—that is, the kind of shift reflected in emphasis on the balance sheet at least on a par with emphasis on the P and L—executive compensation will also have to change. For cash flow and return on assets then become more reliable measurements of performance than earnings per share over a short time period. Stock options, which reward executives for high price-earnings ratios, and which indeed tend to lead managements toward manipulating their businesses for short-term gains and high stock prices, become inappropriate and indeed are at odds with the needs of the business and the judgment of the marketplace.

2.

In the sixties, growth was deified and any growth was good. In the middle seventies, growth, any growth, was widely attacked as evil in itself. But in the years ahead, at least until the babies of the "baby boom" of the fifties have been absorbed into the labor force, if not until they retire forty years hence, a substantial amount of growth will be necessary for minimal economic and social health. And the capital investments needed—in energy, in the environment, in food production and food productivity, in transportation, and so on—are so great in the long run as to make substantial growth appear more probable than zero growth.

But growth is likely to change direction; it has done so after every go-go era. Therefore, management will have to be able to manage the growth of its business and to appraise it, rather than be swayed by every stock market whim or media fashion.

The first thing for management to know is that growth is not something that is desirable. It is a necessity. A business needs to know the minimum of growth without which it would be in danger of becoming marginal in its market. If the market grows, the business must grow too—or else it ceases to be viable and is unable to compete in the long run.

One does not have to be number one. But a company has to have enough of a leadership position in its market not to be squeezed out when a minor setback forces the retailer to cut back the number of appliances he stocks to the two or three or four fast-moving brands. This, in a growing market, requires a growth goal that looks on growth as survival, requiring risk-taking investment at the expense of current earnings.

Equally important will be the ability of management to distinguish between desirable and undesirable growth. Strength and muscle are growth. Growth is strength if it results in overall productivity of the wealth-producing resources of capital, key physical resources, and human resources. Growth that does not make resources more productive is fat and as much a burden on the corporate body as it is on the human body. And growth that is being purchased at the expense of the productivity of the factors of production, as was much of the growth of the go-go years, is a malignant tumor and calls for radical surgery.

3.

There has been increasing concern of late with the multinationals. But the real impact of the emergence of a genuine world economy, of which multinationals are primarily results if not merely symptoms, is still ahead. Increasingly, even managements of small businesses confined to a national or even regional market will have to learn to factor the world economy into their thinking, planning, and decisions.

Since the end of World War II, the economic dynamics have not been based on any one national economy. The motor of economic expansion has been the world economy. And it was the world economy and its forward momentum that again and again during the last twenty-five years bailed out national economies and provided the thrust for the longest sustained period of economic advance in human history.

Any world economy is, however, on a straight collision course with the doctrine of sovereignty, which for almost four hundred years has ruled politics to the point where most of us believe it to be a self-evident axiom. Actually, the assertion of sovereignty, which claims that an economic unit and a political territory should be congruent, was first made in the late sixteenth century. It was then a startling heresy.

In the last thirty years—for the first time in four centuries—the unit of economic action and the unit of political control are again drifting apart. The unit of the economy has become larger and larger, until it can be called a world economy. But political territories in this century have become smaller and more splintered while at the same time more vigorously asserting their sovereignty.

Since 1905, when Norway separated from Sweden, every change of the map has been that of fission of a former political unit to the point where the fewer than forty independent nations of 1914 (more than half of them in the Americas, by the way) have now become almost two hundred sovereign national states.

There is no substitute in sight for the nation state in the political field—but also no substitute for the world economy in the economic field. The next decade, one can predict, will be one of turbulence, of ambivalence on the part of governments. They will want the fruits of the world economy without giving up one iota of their sovereignty. Economics will thus increasingly find itself at loggerheads with politics. The multinational company may well become a victim. It is squarely caught in the middle.

But the world economy will survive, even though it may be a poorer, more dilapidated, greatly hampered world economy. People are not going to lose their vision of the global shopping center— that is, their vision of goods, services, and values for which they strive. Indeed, economically, there are no more distinct cultures, excepting perhaps only Communist China. There are only richer people and poorer people, people who can afford more or less of the same goods and services. And this means that the world economy will continue to provide the economic dynamics for every country.

What does the businessman, therefore, have to know about the world economy? Fifty years ago, businessmen were running regional concerns. Even substantial firms in California or New England did not see that they had to know much about the U.S. economy, and they paid little attention to it until forced to see and to think nationally in the aftermath of the go-go era of the twenties. Now, it is reasonable to predict, they will have to learn to inform themselves similarly about the world economy.

4.

One final thought about the aftermath of any speculative decade: Each has always, in the past, given birth to a new major economic theory. We know we need a new economic theory that focuses on the world economy rather than on the national economy alone. That is, we need a theory that goes beyond the Keynesian apotheosis of national government as all-powerful and all-wise and that comprehends national economics as part of a larger world economy. We need theory focusing on capital formation rather than exclusively on income distribution. We need theory that integrates capital, key physical resources, and human resources with money, credit, and taxes.

Somewhere, today, an economist should be well along toward working out the new theories we need. At least this is the way it has happened in the earlier periods following a go-go decade. But so far neither the new theories nor the equally badly needed new economic policies to be derived from them can be discerned on the horizon.

(1975)

CHAPTER ELEVEN

Managing Capital
Productivity

A HUNDRED YEARS AGO, around 1880, Karl Marx based his prediction of the inevitable and imminent collapse of what we now call "capitalism" or the "free enterprise system" (both terms were not in use until after Marx's death) on the "law" of the diminishing return on capital.

What happened instead is that for a century the productivity of capital in the developed countries—or rather in developed countries with a market economy—was going up except during the most severe depression years. This is one of the major achievements of modern business and the one on which the other achievements perhaps ultimately rest. In part, this achievement was entrepreneurial: the steady shifting of capital from old and rapidly less productive areas of investment into new and more highly productive areas, e.g., into technical or social innovations, which, as Joseph Schumpeter, the great Austro-American economist, convincingly demonstrated seventy years ago, is the true "free capital" of a modern economy.

But the steady increase in the productivity of capital is equally the result of managerial action, of continuing effort to improve the amount of productive work a given unit of capital performs in the business. One example is commercial banking, where one unit of capital today finances many times the volume of transactions it did in Marx's time.

Yet Marx's basic logic was impeccable. If indeed the productivity of capital were to decline inexorably, a system based on market allocation of capital—that is, the free enterprise system—could not survive more than a few short and crisis-ridden decades.

The most disturbing fact in today's world economy may, therefore, be the reversal since the early sixties of the long secular trend toward higher productivity of capital in the developed countries. The downward trend is by no means confined to the free enterprise countries of the West and Japan. It is even more pronounced in the Communist world and especially in Soviet Russia, where, according to all information, the already very low productivity of capital in industry and agriculture has been suffering precipitous and near-catastrophic decline in the last ten to fifteen years. But this is cold comfort for us in the market economies. In a system such as the Soviet economy, where capital is allocated by political fiat rather than by the market, low and declining productivity of capital harms at first only efficiency, living standards, and costs. It need not endanger the system itself for a long time.

The evidence of the last hundred years is, however, quite clear: There is nothing inevitable, nothing inexorable, about the downward trend of capital productivity. Productivity of capital can be maintained and even increased, provided only that businessmen work at it constantly and purposefully.

In fact, working on the productivity of capital is the easiest and usually the quickest way to improve the profitability of a business and the one with the greatest impact. Profit, as the first chapter of any business economics textbook explains, is profit margin multiplied by turnover of capital, that is by productivity of capital. If the profit margin is 6 percent, for instance, and the capital turns over once a year, then there is a 6 percent return on the total capital.

If capital turnover can be raised to 1.2 times a year, total return on capital will go up to 7.2 percent.

To raise profit margins by 20 percent is usually extremely difficult and may be impossible in a competitive market. But to raise capital turnover from once a year to 1.2 times a year often requires only consistent but routine hard work. Indeed, on the basis of quite a few years experience in this field, I am willing to predict that an improvement of this magnitude—that is, an improvement of 20 percent in the productivity of capital over perhaps four or five years—should be available to anyone who seriously tackles the job.

Yet, despite its importance and payoff, not many business managers pay much attention to the productivity of capital, let alone work systematically at raising it. Nor have managers of public-service enterprises such as hospitals paid enough attention to the productivity of capital even though it has fallen a good deal more sharply these last few years in the public-service institution than it has fallen in private business.

One reason, perhaps the single most important one, is that managers, as a rule, get little information on the productivity of capital in their businesses. Most businesses know, of course, how many times a year they turn over their entire capital. But the annual turnover of the company's entire capital in a business, say a paper mill or a department store, is an aggregate. And one cannot manage an aggregate. One always has to manage—and therefore to measure first—major components separately. Yet few managements know what the meaningful components of capital are in their business, let alone what the productivity of capital for each of them is, could be, or should be.

The first step toward managing the productivity of capital is therefore to determine the main areas in one's own company in which capital is actually invested. There rarely are more than a handful. In a typical manufacturing business, for instance, machinery and equipment; inventories of materials, supplies, and finished goods; and receivables usually together account for three quarters of total money invested. In a typical department store there are shelf space (or selling space), receivables, and inventories (inventories in retailing usually have to be subdivided, e.g., into wearing apparel, home furnishings and furniture, appliances, etc., to be meaningful and manageable). How much productive work does the capital employed in each of these areas do? How often does it turn over? How much does it return or contribute? Then one can ask: How much could it and how much should it produce, and what do we have to do to bring this about?

Managements also need to learn a few elementary rules about managing the productivity of capital.

One can increase the productivity of capital in two ways. One can make capital work harder. And one can make it work smarter. This is one of the main reasons, by the way, why the productivity of capital is more easily managed than that of the other two main resources—physical resources and human resources. The productivity of human resources can usually be raised only by making them work smarter; that of physical resources, only by making them work harder.

Locating one's inventory in strategically placed regional warehouses, so that the same amount of inventory can support a larger volume of sales, is making capital work harder. Controlling the product mix to sell a larger proportion of high-contributing products, or a smaller proportion of low-contributing ones, is making capital work smarter. Often one can do both simultaneously. But it is difficult to predict in advance which approach is likely to be appropriate in a given situation, more productive and less risky. Both need to be thought through for each major area of investment in each individual business.

Fixed capital and working capital, while both capital, require different approaches in managing their productivity.

Most businessmen know that nothing is more wasteful in a fixed asset than time not worked. Yet few seem to realize that the standard-cost accounting model assumes—and has to assume—continuous production at a pre-set standard for a given fixed asset, whether a rolling mill in a steel plant, a unit of selling space in a store, or a clinical-care hospital bed. The standard-cost accounting model, in other words, neither measures nor controls the single largest cost of a fixed asset: the cost of capital nonproductivity.

Similarly, cost accounting has to assume a standard product mix, even though both costs and revenues vary tremendously with different mixes (perhaps most for the hospital bed among all major pieces of fixed-capital investment). Managing time-not-worked and product mix are the most effective ways to improve the productivity of capital for most fixed investments. For this, however, one has to *know* first how much time is not being worked and why. One has to know the economics of various product mixes. One has to have economic information in addition to the analytical data of the accounting model. Then one can improve greatly the utilization of time and, with it, the productivity of fixed capital.

But working capital needs to be measured differently and to be managed differently. Unlike fixed assets, it is not "producing" capital but "supporting" capital. The question, therefore, must be asked: What does it, and what should it, support?

Receivables—that is credit extended by a business to its customers —are the obvious example. Companies typically measure their credit management by the proportion of the outstanding loans they collect. "We do a first-rate credit job since our credit losses are less than one percent" is a frequently heard comment. But manufacturers are not in the banking business nor, considering their cost of capital, could they compete with the banks. They give credit to make profitable sales. What then should the objective of a credit policy be in respect to market creation, product introduction, sales, and profits—with low-loss experience as a restraint rather than a goal or measurement? Every business that has asked this question has found (a) that it puts the bulk of its credit where it gets the least back and (b) that it gives the least credit where it gets the most back. Over a three- to four-year period, a business that systematically works on the productivity of the capital employed in receivables can expect that with two thirds of the money now tied up in credit it can finance a larger and more profitable volume of sales.

Finally, few managements seem to know that there are important areas in a business which are not normally considered capital investment—and surely do not appear as such in the balance sheet—but which behave economically very much like fixed capital and have to be managed, above all, for productivity of capital. These are the areas in which *time* is the major cost element, while, over any given period, other costs are relatively fixed and inflexible. Most important among them is the sales force (or the nursing staff in a hospital). This is "fixed human capital." And economically it has to be managed very much as if it were "fixed capital," without any qualifications.

There are great differences in selling ability between salesmen which no amount of training seems to be able to overcome, or even significantly to narrow. But the ablest salesman—or the most dedicated nurse—has only one resource: time. There is a fairly constant relationship between the time a salesman has for sales calls and the number of sales he actually closes. Time not available for work is the major, though usually totally hidden, cost element in these "fixed human assets." And this means that, as in the case of all fixed assets, management first needs to know the productivity of time, and especially how much of the time that should be available for work is actually time not worked and not available for work, and why (e.g., because the salesperson spends two thirds of his or her time on paper work rather than selling). Sometimes it then takes very little change to bring about substantial productivity increases. To put a floor clerk in to take over the paper work has, in some hospitals, for instance, doubled the time nurses have for what they are paid and trained for, and want to do—patient care.

I fully realize that I have oversimplified a complex subject. Productivity is, after all, the combined result of the productivities of all three factors of production: capital, natural resources, and human resources. And it is just as dangerous to increase productivity of capital at the expense of lowering the productivity of the other two factors as it is to increase, say, the productivity of the human resource at the expense of downgrading the productivity of capital (as was done only too often these last twenty-five years).

Finally, I well know that there is a fair number of managers and managements, in small business as well as in large ones, who will, having read this far, say, "What else is new? We have been doing all this and much more for God knows how many years." But these managements constitute, in my experience, a tiny minority even among large, professionally managed companies. Most companies have not even the data for the productivity of capital—and without them one cannot manage.

It is high time that American business managers, in the great majority, learn and accept that managements are paid for managing productivity, especially the productivity of capital, on which, in the last analysis, all other productivities depend; that the productivity of capital can be managed, and that the productivity of capital *must* be managed.

(1975)

CHAPTER TWELVE

Six Durable Economic Myths

THERE IS A GREAT DEAL of talk today about changes that are taking place in the structure of the American economy. But our political rhetoric and our economic policies are dominated by myths about this structure rather than by the structural realities themselves.

In particular there are six such myths believed by almost everyone but completely at odds with the realities of the American economy.

The first of these is the belief, shared by practically all economists as far as I can see, that we face long years of high unemployment, even if the economy returns to "normal."

This simply does not jibe with our population figures. Beginning no later than 1980, we face a very sharp drop in the number of young entrants into the labor force, the result of the "baby bust" that began in 1960 and that lowered the birth figures by 25 percent or more within a very short period. At the same time, for at least another ten years (*1981 note:* that is, until 1990), the number of people who reach retirement age will still go up.

Thus we face long years of a diminishing labor supply, except in the event of a worldwide depression, at least until the mid-nineties, which is the earliest time at which a reversal in the birthrate could have an impact on the size of the labor force. President Ford, in his

Labor Day address in 1975, quoted a figure of 95 million people who will have to have jobs in 1985. But if the President assumed a condition of official "full employment"—or 4 percent unemployed—in that future year, then 95 million people at work ten years hence are hardly more than would have been at work in 1975 if we had 4 percent instead of 9 percent unemployment. The figure which the President cited as an indication of the magnitude of labor force growth turns out to include no labor force growth whatsoever.

The resulting labor tightness will not be felt equally in all areas. Indeed, the area that displayed the greatest manpower shortage in the fifties and sixties—teaching jobs—will continue to be a labor surplus area, again because of the "baby bust" of the last decade. This may explain why the "experts," who are all, or nearly all, university teachers, foresee a continuing labor surplus instead of the reality of an almost certain labor shortage.

The second myth is also closely related to demographics. It is the myth that we can restore high economic activity by reviving consumer demand for the two truly depressed industries of today (1981 note: i.e., 1975)—automobiles and housing. In the very short run this pump-priming may work. For anything longer, say three years or so, demand in these two areas will be low and decline, no matter what economic policies we pursue. The demand will simply not be there.

We have known for fifty years, ever since General Motors made its basic studies in the twenties, that the single most important factor in the demand for new automobiles in the United States is the number of people reaching the age at which they get their drivers' licenses. Of course, they do not, as a rule, buy new cars themselves. They buy the old cars and this enables the former owners of the old cars to buy new cars. And the number of these old-car buyers, beginning in the next year or so, will go down by 25 percent or more and will remain low for the foreseeable future.

Similarly, we have known in respect to housing that it is not "family formation"—that is, the number of men and women who marry (or otherwise take up housekeeping)—but the number of second children born which correlates most closely with demand for new residential housing. And that number, too, is down. All that can be done by pumping money into housing in these circumstances is to drive up the price, which, I suspect, has been the main effect of all the government housing policies all along.

We are not underhoused in this country. We probably have too large a stock of housing, though, of course, it is not all in the places where the people are or want to be. What is needed is a policy that enables people to maintain the value of existing houses, whereas most of our present policy, beginning with rent control and continuing on to the exceedingly high interest rates for housing renewal, has the opposite effect and is—consciously or not—meant to discourage people from maintaining their homes and to encourage them to acquire or build a new one. And that cannot work.

The third myth is that deeply ingrained belief that we, in this country particularly, practice "planned obsolescence" of products—and especially of automobiles. What we have been obsoleting and rapidly is the first owner of a car.

The American automobile, in fact, has a longer working life, measured in miles driven—the only sensible yardstick—than any other automobile. Indeed, the American system, under which people traded in their new car after a year or two, represented, without being planned, the most effective form of income distribution we had in this country—since the first owner paid about twice as much per mile as the third owner (if you include total expenses), so that the poorer people got cars in excellent working condition, good for approximately another 50,000 miles, at a substantially lower price than the first owner paid for what is essentially vanity.

Assuming a new car price of $4,000 (*1981 note:* the price in 1975!), the first owner, driving an average of 10,000 miles a year, pays 28-1/3 cents a mile, consisting of a loss in the car's value of $1,200 and a mileage cost of 13-1/3 cents. The second owner, paying

$2,500 (the dealer taking a slight loss normally) and keeping the car for three years, pays 20 cents a mile (a loss on the car of $2,000, $500 in repairs and 13-1/3 cents a mile). The third and final owner, who pays perhaps $700 and drives 50,000 miles, after which the car is worthless, pays 16 cents a mile.

A more equitable form of income distribution has never been designed. The car itself does not become obsolete; on the contrary, it keeps going on.

My fourth myth would be that basic belief, ingrained in practically all of our economists today, that there is in the American economy, or in any other developed one, a tendency toward over-saving.

This is largely the result of the belief that buying a house, paying Social Security, or contributing to an employee retirement fund is saving. But these are, in effect, transfer payments. The only viable definition of savings is "funds which are available to create jobs." Housing does this to a minimal extent and Social Security not at all. Private pension funds, unless raided by irresponsible and shiftless elements such as have shown themselves in some recent union situations, will accumulate capital for a few more years. But then their pension payments will begin to equal the amounts paid in.

Thus the savings in this country are grossly "undersavings." And we need to think through how to stimulate genuine savings—that is how to form capital available for investment in productive assets (the residential home is not such an asset by the way; it is a durable consumer good).

Fifth, there is the general belief that the corporation income tax is a tax on the "rich" and on the "fat cats." But with pension funds owning 30 percent of American large business—and soon to own 50 percent—the corporation income tax, in effect, eases the load on those in top income brackets and penalizes the beneficiaries of pension funds. In many cases it means an effective tax of almost 50 percent on the retired worker as compared with the 15 percent or less that he is supposed to pay. The corporation income tax has become the most regressive tax in our system, and a tax on the wage earner and on wages. Eliminating it would probably be the single largest step we could take toward greater equality of incomes in this country.

Finally, there is the nice phony figure, believed by everybody and quoted again and again, that the top 5 percent of income earners (those making more than $30,000 or $40,000 a year) own 40 percent of the personal wealth of America. It is, of course, becoming particularly popular as the old figure of "distribution of income" no longer supports those who tell us how terribly unequal American society is.

The joker, of course, is the word "personal." For the single greatest asset of the typical American middle- and working-class family, its future contingent claim on the pension fund of the employing company, is not personal wealth. Nor is it property. But it surely is an asset—and increasingly worth a great deal more than the family home or the family automobile. If it were included, and it is not difficult to do so on a probability and a statistical basis, the distribution of wealth in this country would show a remarkable and progressive equality in which age rather than income is the factor making for inequality.

This adjustment for contingency claims on pension funds would show that the top 5 percent income earners probably own not 40 percent of the wealth of America but no more than 10 percent. Moreover, translating pension expectations into today's values, about 60 percent of the total amount of future pension claims is held by persons in the $9,000 to $20,000 wage bracket. This is by far their biggest asset. Yet, sadly, it is an asset being destroyed very rapidly by the impact of inflation.

These myths are not harmless. They lead to "soak the rich" legislation, which, in effect, then "soaks the poor," the former workers on pensions. They lead to policies enacted as "antirecessionary," which primarily fuel inflation without stimulating consumption or employment. And these myths inhibit the right measures— measures to encourage capital formation. Indeed, unless we discard these myths and face up to economic reality, we cannot hope to have effective economic policies.

(1975)

CHAPTER THIRTEEN

Measuring Business Performance

ONE OF THE BASIC causes of poor performance on the part of analysts, investors, and business managers is the yardstick they use to determine how a business is doing—"earnings per share."

Performance in a business means applying capital productively and there is only one appropriate yardstick of business performance. This is the return on all assets employed or on all capital invested (the two differ, but not significantly). Whether the assets come from the outside or inside makes no difference. Retained earnings are just as much money as a bank loan or new equity. A business that does not earn the going cost of capital on all the money in the business fails to cover its true costs and has an earnings deficiency, whatever its earnings per share.

The return on assets must include all moneys available to service capital. This includes not only profits from which dividends can be paid, but also all interest charges on all debt. It includes depreciation, which does not figure in earnings per share, but it excludes inventory profits, which frequently do, depending on a company's accounting practices.

These are the measures that make economic sense. If investment flows to companies with high returns by these yardsticks, the economy's performance will be optimized. These are the measures of the economic regulating function usually assigned to "profits."

What then are the "earnings per share" that companies and their accountants grind out so regularly and publicize so mightily? The conventional "earnings per share" figure not only doesn't measure corporate performance but it rarely even measures true "earnings per share." The term is a misnomer. What it really represents is "taxable earnings." It is what is left after all the charges the tax collector accepts as deductible. But this is a purely arbitrary figure that has little or nothing to do with economic performance.

"Earnings per share" as reported are practically never what people think they are, that is "earnings available to the shareholder." If they were, companies could and would distribute most or all in the form of dividends—and practically no company does. Before one can really know what a company has truly earned on its equity capital, he therefore has to correct the reported figures for those capital charges, which, while genuine costs, are not accepted as tax deductible by the tax collector and are therefore included in reported "earnings per share." This requires starting out with return on assets or on total capital employed. Only this figure shows what capital charges are needed over and above those which the tax collector accepts.

There are four such genuine capital charges—each a true cost, even if included in the reported earnings figure. The first is deficiency of revenue as measured against the *cash needs* ahead—the only area, by the way, to which analysts pay much attention. A business that cannot provide out of its revenues for the foreseeable cash needs of operations, including service on its debt, does not earn enough.

A business, secondly, must earn the *going cost of capital* on all the money in the business. A company which shows high "earnings per share" because, for example, it still enjoys the benefits of the lower interest rates of the past is using up capital and reporting it as earnings. Such a business cannot raise money without depressing its earnings. But sooner or later—and usually sooner—the low-cost capital has to be replaced; and then the going cost of capital has to be paid. A gain resulting from low money costs of the past should go into a reserve rather than into earnings. It does not truly reflect the company's profitability.

The third adjustment is the provision for known and foreseeable *risks*. This is a genuine cost, as is any insurance premium. The most common risk is the cyclical one. It is a known and foreseeable hazard and has high probability. One year's earnings, like any one monthly or quarterly figure, are therefore by themselves misleading unless adjusted for a cyclical period. Another typical risk for which earnings need to be adjusted is the high risk of overexposure and vulnerability after a period of rapid growth. It is prudent to assume that even a slight setback after such a period will reduce sales to where they would have been if the company or the industry had grown throughout the period at a rate somewhat between that of the lowest year in the period and the average year. This formula, though quite unscientific, fits remarkably well with actual experience—that of the mobile-home industry, for instance, in the sixties and early seventies. And then one adjusts earnings to the most probable long-term figure, considering the risk of growth in order to have a reliable measurement of business or industry performance.

Finally, the "earnings per share" figure needs to be adjusted to account for the known and foreseeable needs of the business. One of them is the need to provide for the growth required to maintain a company's market position in an expanding market or its technological leadership in an expanding and changing technology. A company that fails to do so endangers its very survival. A second such need is protection of capital against the ravages of inflation. Depreciation surely has to be adjusted to inflation rather than be based on historical cost.

All this was known seventy-five years ago. "I never listen to the securities analysts—I listen to the credit analysts," Bernard Baruch is reputed to have said when asked to explain his performance as Wall Street's biggest and boldest speculator in the early decades of this century. Fifty years ago the DuPont Company codified this knowledge in its famous "return on investment" charts, around which the DuPont management was organized.

But the definitive work on earnings, on costs of capital, and on measuring economic performance has been done in the last thirty years by a whole generation of business economists.

As a result of this work, we know that "assets employed" or "capital invested" mean precisely what the words say. Whether the money has been put into buildings or into receivables is irrelevant; there are different uses for money, but no different money. Whether the money is equity or loans also makes no difference, nor does it matter that the money invested is "our own" rather than raised on the outside. Earning power and, above all, "earnings per share" are seriously damaged—and very soon—if retained earnings are invested at a lower rate than the full cost of outside capital.

We further know what to include in "return on capital" or "return on assets." Since the purpose is to measure the economic performance of a business, all moneys available to service capital are part of "return." This includes all interest charges on all debt, depreciation (which in economic terms is essentially nontaxable return), as well as what is traditionally considered "earnings on equity capital." It does not, however, include profits which do not reflect the earning power of the business. Inventory losses are genuine losses. But inventory profits do not belong in "return on assets" or in "return on capital employed." Other nonrecurring gains incidental to the business, such as a gain from selling a plant, are also not part of "return on capital employed"—except in a company whose business it is to buy and sell plants.

Return on all assets or on all capital investment is not the only yardstick available in measuring the performance of a business.

Indeed, every business might well use a second one. In a manufacturing business, for instance, return on "value added in manufacturing"—that is on the difference between revenue on goods sold and money paid out for supplies and materials—is an important measurement. It is very sensitive and a "leading indicator," which tends to go up or down before returns on total capital invested or on assets employed show significant changes. For a retail business, return on selling space is similarly an important indicator of performance.

But these additional measurements have to fit the individual business. The "value added" yardstick makes sense only for businesses that are truly manufacturing businesses. Also, this second yardstick is usually available only to the insider and rarely to an outsider.

Though many business executives are skeptical of the accuracy of "earnings per share" as a business measurement, they often say, "What choice do we have? The market uses this measure whether it makes sense or not." But this is a half-truth at best. Witness the enormous differences in "price-earnings ratios." The main reason is that the stock market tends to value a stock primarily on the basis of a rough guess at total return rather than on the basis of the highly publicized and visible "earnings per share" figure. Despite its follies, foibles, and fashions, the stock market is a good deal more rational than the "experts," at least over any extended period of time.

The best examples of this were the stock prices during the acquisition binge of the late sixties. A good many of the "conglomerateurs" played the "earnings per share" game and structured the purchases of an acquisition in such a way as to show increased "per share earnings" even though total returns did not go up and often went down. The people who sold their businesses against what eventually came to be known as "Chinese money" all lost heavily in the end—unless they immediately sold the securities they got. The stock market speedily adjusted the share price to the actual returns on capital rather than to reported per share earnings.

Thus there is something to the old-fashioned belief that the stock price reflects the discounted value of future dividends, that is, the present value of future earnings actually available for distribution.

It is possible, with a little work and ingenuity, to determine with adequate probability the return performance of publicly owned companies. But it might not be a bad idea for companies to provide the necessary information themselves. The demand for "full disclosure" increasingly focuses on the economic prospects of a company and on its economic performance—that is, on the extent to which it actually produces wealth out of the resources entrusted to it.

The key figure for this is return on all assets (or on capital employed) related to cash needs, to cost of capital, to risks and needs. This rather than the meaningless "earnings per share" figure is what the public, the SEC, the analysts, and, above all, the stockholders should expect—and might demand—from a company's published accounts and annual statements.

And it is this figure that should provide the link between business performance and executive compensation. It is legitimate and desirable to relate executive rewards to company performance— but it had better be true performance. To tie compensation to reported "earnings per share" subordinates performance to appearances. It may even reward executives for milking rather than building a company.

(1976)

CHAPTER FOURTEEN

Why Consumers Aren't Behaving

EVERYBODY KNOWS HOW THE CONSUMER ought to behave, except the consumer.

Everybody knows, for instance, that the first thing consumers cut back, at the slightest hint of economic trouble, is eating out. We have now (i.e., in 1976) been through two, if not three, years of fairly serious economic turbulence—whether you call it a "severe recession" or a "mild depression." Yet consumer buying of prepared meals, in the form of restaurant meals, at such convenience food stores as McDonald's or Kentucky Fried Chicken, or in the form of fully prepared dinners ready to be heated and served, has been going straight up. In fact, a good many people in the food business predict that by 1985 every other meal consumed in this country, including breakfast, will be bought as a fully prepared meal, to be consumed in a restaurant, in a drive-in, or at home.

Similarly, everybody knows that in a recession the demand for expensive and big houses drops sharply while the demand for small houses goes up sharply. But when the housing industry, responding to this, introduced what it called "basic houses," that is houses at a relatively low price and about as well equipped as standard houses were in the mid-fifties, nobody wanted them.

Very much the same thing has been happening to cars. For fifty years GM has called every marketing turn in the automobile market—but not this time. This time GM anticipated that buyers would shift to smaller cars—the only rational expectation in view of the sharp drop in employment and income, and considering the parallel very sharp increase in the operating cost of an automobile as a result of the jump in gasoline prices. But the public buys big cars. The "hot car" of this year (i.e., 1976) is a new "moderately priced" $15,000 Cadillac.

Business travel on scheduled airlines flights did indeed go down very sharply with the recession and came back directly parallel to the recovery. But air travel as a whole showed no such "proper" behavior. Chartered travel of all sorts has been going up quite steadily. It shows great price sensitivity in that fluctuations in the foreign value of the dollar directly translate themselves into changes in demand for charter-flight destinations. But total demand for package tours has been doing well all along.

These are just illustrations. Many industries that market consumer goods report similar "abnormal" behavior. There seems to be no pattern, except that the pattern we expect to see is not the dominant pattern at all. In some classes of expenditures, consumers apparently spend much less than they "should"; in others, much more; and in some, exactly what marketing theory and folklore expect them to spend.

The instances of "abnormal" consumer behavior may be pure coincidence. They can all probably be explained away. And this is the way most businessmen I know react to consumer behavior that surprises them.

One explanation that some thoughtful people in business offer is that this behavior indicates "stagflation"—that is, public response to an economy which simultaneously stagnates and suffers fairly severe inflation. One cannot dismiss this explanation out of hand.

There are some indications that continual expectations of inflation play a part, perhaps even a substantial part, in the consumer's behavior. They may explain, for instance, the tremendous boom in luxury homes or the continued appreciation in the price of top-flight jewelry and of "really first-rate" art objects. The people who buy these things are the same people who traditionally bought common shares as a "hedge against inflation" and who then bought gold for the same reason.

The stagflation explanation does not, however, explain a good deal of observed behavior. It does not explain, for instance, why retail sales of standard consumer goods—the things people normally buy—have been so sluggish, especially in 1975 and 1976.

Such sales should have gone up fairly fast in a period in which people do not trust the purchasing power of money and expect prices to go up steadily. Similarly, the high savings rate of 1975–76 was hardly compatible with stagflation; nor was the influx of money into savings institutions, even though interest rates were then falling.

An alternative explanation, therefore, needs to be considered: The American consumer market is undergoing a new segmentation. There is evidence for this. In effect, three groups are emerging as dominant market forces. The traditional marketing theory does not take them into account and they behave differently from the standard model, if only because their economic reality is quite different.

The first of these groups is older people, especially people who are retired. In percentages, this is the most rapidly growing group in the American population. It now comprises some 30 million people—as against 94 million people in the work force. In another few years it will have grown to 40 million people, while the work force will have grown to only 100 million people.

The retired people are not much affected by unemployment. They are protected to a fair extent against inflation with Social Security and, increasingly, private pension plans escalating to keep in step with inflation and the cost of living. Contrary to general belief, the older people aren't all poor and don't all have low incomes.

As a result, retirees are not just customers for hearing aids or wheelchairs. They are, first of all, customers for such things as the leisurely vacation, for they have plenty of time. They are customers for recreation vehicles. And they are very heavy customers for pre-pared food, in part because going out to the fried-chicken parlor is one way to break the monotony of an idle day. Maybe 10 million to 15 million of the 30 million in the older population today are poor, or at least have low incomes. But this leaves another 15 million who are "affluent" without being rich. And tomorrow, when there will be 40 million of the older people, the affluent consumer group among them is likely to be 25 million people or so—and this is a large market segment indeed.

The second such new group may be the young adults. In actual numbers they are growing faster than retirees, though they are growing somewhat less fast in percentages. Fifty percent or so of these young adults—that is of the people who are now entering the labor force in large numbers—have sat in class rooms beyond high school. One hears a great many scare stories about the Ph.D. who cannot find a job and drives a cab. But actually, the highly schooled among the young adults have a low unemployment rate and very high incomes. Starting salaries for young adults have not gone down at all, despite the tremendous number who are being graduated.

This group appears to be heavily influenced by inflationary expectations. Their savings rate is low and as buyers they are shift-ing strongly toward the "big ticket" item. For example, they buy expensive homes, considering their incomes. They take expensive skiing trips. They own boats.

Finally, there are the married working women, probably the most important of the "new" groups. Half of the married women in this country now hold jobs. It's also in this group that the greatest additional growth in jobholders and earnings is likely to occur; it is the only group in which there is a sizable reservoir of employable people.

The husband is still considered the breadwinner, and his income is used for normal household expenses. The wife's income averages about 60 percent of the husband's and is used for "extras." Her money provides the margin for a bigger house, the luxury car, the expensive vacation. But the household spending pattern, based on the husband's income, remains sensitive to consumer confidence and to expectations about job security and income. The general budget of the two-breadwinner family isn't greatly affected by the wife's earnings, which are considered "extraordinary" earnings and are used for "extraordinary" purchases.

Twice since World War I there have been profound changes in the American marketplace. In the early 1920s, the American mass market emerged; Alfred Sloan was among the first to understand this, and he built General Motors on market segmentation by income groups. Then, about 1950, there emerged a market segmented by "life-style"; such things as education, age and number of children, and location of home became as important as, and perhaps more important than, income in determining consumer patterns.

Now we may be witnessing a new segmentation by population dynamics. The older person, the young adult, the mature married female worker may all emerge as distinct consumer segments that will cause marketing men to rewrite their rules of how consumers ought to behave. Such groups behave "rationally." But what for one market segment is rational—i.e., makes the most of its economic conditions—makes little sense for the other group.

It's risky, of course, to predict structural economic changes in American society. It's perfectly possible that the puzzling consumer behavior of the last few years will in another few years be seen as nothing but minor and irrelevant coincidences. But there is also a possibility that something fundamental is happening to consumer behavior. At the very least, it bears careful watching.

(1976)

CHAPTER FIFTEEN

Good Growth and Bad Growth

ALMOST EVERY BUSINESS DESIRES to grow. And most proclaim that they will grow. But only a handful have a growth policy, let alone a growth strategy. And even fewer know whether they are really growing or whether they are merely getting obese.

Growth does not, however, happen because business desires it. By itself, there is no virtue in business growth. A company is not necessarily better because it is bigger, any more than the elephant is better because it is bigger than the honeybee. A business has to be the right size for its market, its economy, and its technology; and the right size is whatever produces the optimal yield from productive resources.

But business is always the wrong size, no matter how small or how big it is, if it is marginal in its market. That the market leader enjoys disproportionate profitability—as the now popular theory of the Boston Consulting Group asserts—does not hold true for every industry and every market. Book publishing, for instance, is a clear exception.

But the marginal business, no matter how large, suffers disproportionate lack of profitability, and—even more dangerous—tends to fall behind further and further with every turn of the business cycle. No business can afford to slide for lack of adequate growth into the marginal position into which Chrysler deteriorated in the world's automobile markets.

The first question to ask in a growth policy is, therefore, not "How much growth do we want?" It is "How much growth do we need so as not to become marginal as our market grows?" The answer is by no means easy, and it is always controversial. It depends on how a management defines its company's market. It also depends on industry structure. An adequate, if not a leadership, position in one industry is marginal in another. And market definition and industry structure have a habit of changing, often quite fast and drastically, as the size of the market or the appropriate technologies change.

Still, unless a business knows its minimum growth goal, it has no growth policy. And in all probability, until it knows its minimum growth goal it will not have much real growth either.

But a business then needs to think through its growth strategy. The first step in a growth strategy is not to decide where and how to grow. It is to decide what to abandon. In order to grow, a business must have a systematic policy to get rid of the outgrown, the obsolete, the unproductive. The foundation of a growth strategy is the freeing of resources for new opportunities. This requires withdrawing resources from the areas, products, services, markets, and technologies where results can no longer be obtained or where the returns on efforts are rapidly diminishing. A growth strategy begins with asking every two or three years, "If we did not already produce this product line or did not already serve this market, would we now, knowing what we know now, go into it?"

If the answer is "no," one does not say, "Let's make another study." One says, "How can we get out or at least stop throwing additional resources in?"

Growth comes from exploiting opportunity. One cannot exploit opportunity if productive resources, and especially the scarce resource of performing people, are committed to keeping yesterday alive a little longer, to defending the obsolete, and to making alibis for the unproductive and the things that should have worked but did not. Strategic planning of the most successful companies—an IBM, a Xerox, a GE, for instance—starts with the assumption that the most successful products of today are the ones which are likely to obsolete the fastest tomorrow—and it is a realistic assumption.

A growth strategy further requires concentration. The greatest mistake in a growth strategy, and the most common one, is to try to grow in too many areas. A growth strategy has to center on the targets of opportunity—that is, the areas in which a specific company's strength are most likely to produce extraordinary results. First, a look should be taken at markets, population, economy, society, and technology—to identify the most probable changes and their direction. In fact, one best starts out by asking, "What changes have already occurred that are most likely to have long-range impact?"

Changes in demographics are, of course, always the most reliable index, for the lead times of population changes are both thoroughly known and inexorable. Nearly everyone in the American labor force of the year 2000, whether American-born or born elsewhere, is alive by now, for instance. Changes in knowledge, perception, and the application of new science or insight also have fairly well-known and predictable lead times.

More important perhaps than the ability to anticipate changes is the realization that change creates opportunity and that businessmen are being paid to convert social, economic, and technological change into profitable business opportunities. The last step in formulating a growth strategy is to think through what the specific strengths of *our* business are, the specific contributions customers pay *our* business for, the specific things *we* do well—and then focus them on the anticipated changes to identify a company's priority opportunities. It is only too common for a business to define "opportunity" as something that happens on the outside. Opportunities are what a specific business makes happen—and this means fitting a company's specific excellence to the changes in marketplace, population, economy, society, technology, and values.

Finally, a growth policy needs to be able to distinguish between healthy growth, fat, and cancer—all three are "growth," but surely all three are not equally desirable. The ability to distinguish between healthy growth and deleterious, if not degenerative, growth is particularly important in an inflationary time such as ours. Inflation distorts. And it distorts, above all, the meaning of volume figures and of growth statistics. A lot of growth in an inflationary period is pure fat. But some of it is also precancerous.

Volume by itself, in other words, is no indication of growth. It first needs to be adjusted for inflation. And then it needs to be analyzed as to its quality. Growth that is pure volume is not "growth" at all—it is simply so much delusion. Larger volume is healthy only if it produces higher overall productivity of all productive resources combined—capital, key physical resources, time, and people. And if growth brings about greater overall productivity, if in other words it is healthy growth, it is the duty of management to support it.

If growth does not improve the productivity of resources overall, but also does not downgrade it, it is fat. It then needs to be watched carefully. It often is necessary to support volume that does not lead to increased productivity for a short time. But if, after two or three years, additional volume is just volume without improved productivity, it should be considered fat. It should be sloughed off, lest it become a burden on the system. And growth that results in a decrease in the total productivity of a company's resources, except for the shortest of start-up periods, should be considered as precancerous and treated through radical surgery.

In the late sixties at the height of the go-go frenzy, any business was expected to grow forever. This was inane; nothing can grow forever. Then, in the early seventies, zero growth became fashionable. Of course, there is a very real possibility of a worldwide depression resulting from more than fifteen years of worldwide inflation.

Actually the years of the zero growth trend of the seventies were years of very real and fast growth. But the growth in these years was largely in new areas, both in respect to technology and products, and in respect to geography. It was not, as a whole, a continuation of the growth of the twenty-five years since 1948, that is, after the Marshall Plan had ushered in the world's longest and largest economic growth period.

It is, in other words, irrational not to plan for growth. But to plan, as do so many of our businesses, on continuation of the growth of the post-World War II period may be even more irrational still. Today every business needs a growth goal, a growth strategy, and ways to distinguish healthy growth from fat and cancer.

(1979)

CHAPTER SIXTEEN

The "Re-Industrialization" of America

WE'LL HEAR MORE AND MORE these next few years about "re-industrializing America," that is, about restoring the country's competitive strength and leadership in manufacturing industry. Both major parties were working on re-industrialization planks in their platforms for the 1980 presidential campaign. And there is a similar demand for re-industrialization policies in Japan, Germany, Britain, Sweden, and other developed industrial countries.

It is important, however, to distinguish between two meanings of the slogan. When union leaders and executives in old-line manufacturing industries call for re-industrialization they most commonly mean policies that will maintain traditional blue-collar employment—especially jobs for semiskilled machine operators—in traditional mass-production industries.

But in the United States and in all other highly developed industrial countries, including the more industrialized parts of the Communist bloc, policies aimed at maintaining traditional blue-collar employment are incompatible with another meaning of re-industrialization: the restoration of the country's international competitiveness to produce and export manufactured goods. On the contrary, the only way for a developed economy such as the United States' to regain its international competitiveness is to encourage a fairly rapid shrinkage of traditional blue-collar employment.

The reason for this paradox is demography, not technology. Most developed countries are beginning to experience their second major demographic transition in this century. The first one, beginning around the turn of the century and cresting after World War II, was the shift from farming to manufacturing industry as the center of employment.

The movement of large masses from the farm to the plant created the modern blue-collar worker, i.e., the semiskilled machine operator, and with him mass-production industry. Farm labor forces were decimated. Farmers made up 60 percent of the total U.S. work force in 1900, but account for only 3 percent to 4 percent today, while the proportion in Japan dropped from 60 percent as late as 1946 to less than 10 percent today. But the demographic shift enabled both farm output and industrial output to triple or quadruple.

Now the second demographic transition is moving labor massively out of manual work into "knowledge work." Compared with thirty years ago, only half as many young people in the United States are coming into the labor force with the schooling, expectations, and skills that will lead them into traditional blue-collar work. The squeeze will become even tighter when the "baby bust" children of the sixties and seventies reach working age: Only one third as many potential blue-collar entrants will be available in 1990 as there were in 1950.

The demographic shift in the industrialized countries is inextricably linked to transformations in the developing economies, which are now going through the same transition from farm to city that took place in the developed economies earlier. Thanks to this transition and to a sharp drop in infant mortality since 1950, most developing countries now have a tremendous bulge of young people qualified only for traditional labor-intensive, low-skilled, or semi-skilled, machine work. Even with productivity miracles, there is no way that semiskilled workers in the industrial countries can compete with low-wage labor in countries like Malaysia, Mexico, and mainland China with their 40 percent to 50 percent unemployment rates and their millions of young urban semiskilled workers.

To maintain competitive strength and leadership in manufacturing, whether in competition with Germany and Japan or with the rapidly industrializing countries of the Third World, therefore requires a country like America to gear manufacturing technology to the available labor supply of knowledge workers rather than to the dwindling supply of manual blue-collar workers. It requires shifting manufacturing work from operating machines to programing machines, and indeed to programing plants and processes rather than individual machines or lines.

Most of all, perhaps, it requires a shift in managerial attitude. Labor must be treated not as a cost (a view which is anyhow incompatible with true productivity) but as a resource. For in terms of cost, labor in the developed countries cannot possibly be productive and competitive.

There are three parallel approaches to this kind of re-industrialization. The one that has been attracting the most attention over the last twenty-five years is automation, especially the use of robots, or fully automated machine tools, on the assembly line. Sophisticated robots are already being used in the automobile industry, particularly in the Zama plant of Nissan, the manufacturer of Datsun cars, as well as in some General Motors assembly plants in the United States.

But however spectacular robots may appear to the layman, they are probably a good deal less important than a second approach to re-industrialization: the redesign of entire plants and entire processes as integrated flow systems. This redesign barely affects conventional assembly but totally changes the manufacture of parts and their quality control, which are integrated and constantly calibrated by feedback from the end product. The Japanese TV manufacturers use this approach in their American plants. So does RCA, whose TV plants in the United States are capable of competing with offshore low-wage producers and beating them handsomely.

The third and most important approach to re-industrialization is the integration of the mini-computer and micro-computer into the machine, the tool, the instrument. This development is proceeding so fast and furiously that some observers speak of a "third industrial revolution." Its impact is fully comparable to that of the fractional horsepower motor one hundred years ago.

Within thirty years the fractional horsepower motor transformed the industrial landscape and made possible today's manufacturing technology, today's farming, and today's household appliances. Similarly, the integration of mini-computer into machine and tool shifts workers from being "semiskilled" blue-collar machine operators to being "semiknowing" white-coated technicians.

Demographic pressures are so great and so irreversible that they will render futile any policy that tries to maintain traditional blue-collar employment in the traditional manufacturing plant. Even in the short run such a policy can only diminish the number of blue-collar jobs, no matter how much money might be spent on creating and maintaining them. For it could only make traditional manufacturing industries less competitive.

The opposite course would be to maximize knowledge jobs, encouraging automation and the shift from blue-collar workers to white-coated technicians and easing the hardships of old blue-collar workers by redundancy planning. The shift to knowledge-based manufacturing is the only way to expand employment in this country without worsening inflation.

But can any politician in any of the developed countries advocate it? The best we can hope for would be a re-industrialization policy that emulates American farm policy since the days of Franklin Roosevelt.

For fifty years now our farm rhetoric has trumpeted as its goal the maintenance of the small-family farmer. But by and large, farm policies have given priority to making farming competitive rather than to protecting inefficient farmers. Or at least our farm policies have confined themselves to paying off the inefficient farmer rather than yielding policy substance to him. Whether the politicians and farm leaders always knew what they were doing, I doubt. But in general they understood the demographic transition and saw it as an opportunity.

Will we likewise use the second demographic transition as an opportunity for a true re-industrialization of America?

(1980)

CHAPTER SEVENTEEN

The Danger of Excessive Labor Income

IT IS RAPIDLY BECOMING CLEAR that both productivity and capital formation depend heavily on the labor-income ratio—the proportion of value added that goes to wages and fringe benefits—and that this is true whether we are talking about a company, an industry, or a national economy. If the ratio goes above a certain threshold, apparently between 80 percent and 85 percent, productivity declines and capital formation falls too low to maintain present jobs, let alone create new ones.

Consider the U.S. auto and steel industries. It is common today to bemoan the decline of American industrial competitiveness and to wonder what has become of American management. In truth, however, the "American disease" is by and large confined to autos and steel.

The bulk of U.S. manufacturing industry—from fashion goods to airplanes, from textiles to computers—has been enjoying an extraordinary export boom these last four years, almost as vigorous as the export boom immediately after World War II when the industrial plants of our potential competitors lay in ruins. The export performance of most American industry explains why the much-heralded 1979–80 "recession" was so much shorter and milder than anticipated—despite oil-price jumps and the near collapse of the auto and steel industries. Indeed, our export *surplus* with the Common Market will most likely be one of the major problems of foreign economic relations for the Reagan Administration.

Autos and steel, thought to be the rule, are thus truly the exception. And they are the exception principally because they spend too much, relatively, on wages and fringe benefits. In most American manufacturing the labor-income ratio is probably still below 80 percent (though reliable data are hard to come by). But in autos and steel the ratio is well above 85 percent and may approach 90 percent.

Labor costs in the U.S. auto and steel industries—whether measured per employee, per hour actually worked, or per unit of output—are 50 percent to 100 percent higher than the prevailing labor costs of other *American* manufacturing industries. At Ford Motor Company, the hourly labor cost per employee, including all fringes and the costs of not working, e.g., absenteeism, is close to $25, compared with about $15 even in high-paying industries such as chemical manufacturing. Since the labor costs of Japanese and German auto- and steel-makers are roughly on a par with prevailing American labor costs in *other* manufacturing industries, it's no wonder that the U.S. auto and steel industries have had so much trouble competing against imports—and that so many auto and steelworkers are out of a job.

Apart from worsening import competition, a labor-income ratio of 85 to 90 percent makes capital formation impossible and thus endangers the jobs of tomorrow. Even General Motors is barely able to generate or raise the sums needed to modernize its plants and convert them to the production of fuel-efficient cars.

In Europe, Ford has already done a superb job producing and marketing competitive, fuel-efficient small cars. But in this country it cannot generate the capital fast enough to change its plants to producing cars it already makes, cars that have been proven in the market. The steel companies are in the same boat, and in such circumstances it makes little difference how good management is, how well it is planning, and how well it can design and market.

On the economy-wide level, too, countries where labor income accounts for more than 85 percent of gross national product—Britain, the Netherlands, Belgium, and Scandinavia—are in the deepest trouble. By contrast, the Germans and Japanese operate on labor-income ratios of 70 to 75 percent, or at most 80 percent.

Indeed, the labor-income ratio seems to be more important for the ability of a country to perform than is the proportion of GNP that goes through the transfer mechanism of government. In Germany the transfer proportion is high, in Japan it is quite low. Yet both economies perform somewhat alike, and far better than countries such as the United States, where the transfer proportion is comparatively low but where key industries have a high labor-income ratio.

Economists and economic policy-makers have traditionally paid little attention to the labor-income ratio, for the simple reason that it never was a problem before. The relationship between "wage fund" and "capital fund" has been studied and argued about for almost two hundred years, since David Ricardo's first theoretical papers. But right down to John Maynard Keynes, the central question was always how to prevent the "capital fund" from becoming "excessive." But now, with a labor-income ratio of 80 to 85 percent, even convinced Keynesians accept the idea that economic theory and economic policy have to concern themselves with restoring productivity and capital formation.

High labor-income ratios also pose a life-or-death crisis for the labor union and for traditional wage setting through collective bargaining. It is no coincidence that the two U.S. industries—autos and steel—in so much trouble, with so much unemployment, are the two industries where there is a virtual labor union monopoly, with practically no nonunion plants.

What's more, a labor-income ratio of 80 to 85 percent invalidates all the fundamental tenets of the labor movement—e.g., the axiom that the labor share of GNP can never be excessive. When the labor movement started, well over one hundred years ago, labor's share of GNP was at most 40 percent or so. Hence, Samuel Gompers, the pioneering leader of American labor, defined the aim of labor as "More."

But can this aim still be maintained when labor income is 85 percent of national product and there is no more "more"? Or does one then have to ask what limits have to be set on labor income as a share of gross product to enable a company, an industry, or a country to form enough capital for the jobs of tomorrow?

It has similarly been a tenet of the labor movement that a union monopoly—unlike a business monopoly—can never do damage. A business monopoly, Adam Smith pointed out, reduces aggregate demand and thereby creates unemployment. By contrast, labor economists have been arguing for a century that a union monopoly can only create demand, i.e., purchasing power, and therefore will not promote unemployment. Even most pro-business economists have accepted this, excepting only a few American heretics, such as George Stigler and the late Henry Simons, both at the University of Chicago. But surely in the U.S. auto and steel industries, union monopoly has helped create massive unemployment.

Unions, finally, have argued since well before Marx that the worker's propensity to save would go up at least as fast as his income. Capital formation in a society of low surplus—that is, little income other than labor income—would be no lower and, the argument ran, probably higher than in a society where capital formation is in the hands of capitalists or of business. In postulating the multiplier effect of consumption demand on investment, Keynes gave only an elegant theoretical formulation to what had long been an axiom among socialists and labor economists.

But can any of these axioms still be maintained? Or will we have to replace them by totally different postulates? One might be that labor income has to be kept below a certain point, say 80 to 85 percent, if a company, an industry, or a country is to be sure of adequate capital formation. Perhaps we should limit union monopoly powers to enable industries dominated by unions to maintain their competitive position as well as their ability to create future jobs.

We might also have to balance every increase in the share of labor income with measures to stimulate capital formation, especially in businesses—whether that means a shift from taxes on higher incomes to sales taxes, for instance, or the removal of taxes on savings, capital gains, and business profits. Maybe we will even have to make acceptance of a rise in the labor-income ratio dependent on the capital formation rate—or link the two in some way which does not, as Keynesians and Friedmanites both do, rely entirely on the invisible hand of a multiplier which automatically turns consumer demand or money supply into investment.

The union crisis is the most difficult of all challenges: a crisis of success. The labor union has attained its objectives—and when that happens, institutions tend to become reactionary and then degenerate and atrophy.

As events in Poland in 1980 have shown again, a modern society needs the labor union. There has to be a countervailing power against the power of the bosses—even in a free economy where the market sets severe limits to the power of the bosses. But countervailing power is still power. And to be legitimate, power requires what the union so far lacks: clear responsibility, accountability, and pre-set limitations.

(1981)

PART III

The Non-Profit Sector

Most people do not hear "management"; they hear "business management." Management as a function, as an organ of authority and responsibility, and as a discipline was indeed first seen, identified, and studied as a part of business enterprise. But this is hardly more than a historical—and primarily American—accident. Management is the specific organ of any modern institution. The people in management may be called by different names—schools and hospitals, for instance, prefer to speak of administrators. But what all of them do is to manage. What all of them practice is management.

And the non-business institutions, and especially those of the Third Sector—that is non-businesses which are not governments, whether privately or publicly owned—have been the true growth area of a modern society. Indeed, about half of the students who receive an MBA from American graduate business schools do not go to work for businesses but for the Third Sector.

But the Third Sector organizations—schools; hospitals; community organizations, whether the Ford Foundation or the Boy Scouts, the Red Cross, or the art museum; labor unions and churches; accounting firms and the large law firms; and countless associations of all kinds—professional and industrial, learned, and recreational—have also changed out of all recognition. The hospital, only a short hundred years ago, was still the place for the poor to die.

In the years ahead, Third Sector institutions are certain to face more rather than less challenge. Many of the needs of the Third Sector institution are the same as those of the business enterprise: Both need accounting, both employ people, both need marketing. But there are also specific Third Sector needs and specific Third Sector performances. They are the concern of the pieces in this section.

CHAPTER EIGHTEEN

Managing the Non-Profit Institution

FIFTEEN YEARS AGO APPLICANTS for entrance positions as overseas field representatives of a major U.S.-based charity were routinely asked, "Do you have enough of a private income to work for a non-profit institution?" For thirty years, until he retired in 1978, the organization's executive director refused to accept for himself more than $20,000 a year in salary although the charity had grown into a $100 million enterprise. Today the same organization pays the MBAs whom it now recruits a salary of $21,500 and living expenses abroad the first year. And the successor of the old executive director makes $75,000 a year plus bonus.

When Thomas Hoving left the directorship of New York's Metropolitan Museum of Art in the spring of 1978, the board, deciding that the job had become too big for one man, split it into two, a president-chief executive officer and a director-chief artistic officer. Each position was reported to pay a six-figure salary.

A former student of mine, aged thirty-three, recently moved from assistant vice president-operations of a middle-sized bank to executive director of a suburban county medical society. He heads a full-time staff of thirty-five and is being paid $45,000 a year. In the early 1960s when his physician father served as the unpaid secretary-treasurer of the same society, it had one full-time employee, a woman clerk making $8,000 a year, with the young wife of a physician member editing the newsletter part-time for $50 a month.

Everybody knows that hospitals have exploded in personnel, wages, complexity, patient load, range of services, and costs. But many other service institutions have grown at similar rates in their employment, their complexity, and their costs. Service institutions now pay salaries that are fully competitive with government jobs (though service employees often don't think so) as well as with all but the top positions in big business. And the demands on service personnel have not only grown fast—they have changed dramatically.

Fifteen years ago, for instance, the Seattle Art Museum, known for its first-rate oriental collections, considered 100,000 visitors a big year. By mid-November of 1978 when the King Tut exhibition closed a four-month run in Seattle it had attracted more than one million visitors to the museum—almost all of them people who fifteen years ago would never have dreamed of going there.

Service institutions have grown so big that they may now employ more people than federal, state, and local government put together. And they are so important that we are beginning to talk of a Third Sector of society—neither public (governmental) nor private in the old sense of the private business sector. The Third Sector is composed of institutions which are not government agencies but which are still not profit-making. Yet so far we have paid little attention to the Third Sector and its economics, management, performance, and impact.

One reason for this is that the Third Sector is such a mixed lot. It includes hospitals, museums, universities, libraries, and symphony orchestras; thousands of industry or trade associations, chambers of commerce, professional bodies like the bar associations or the registered nurses; civic groups like the Boy Scouts and religious ones like the Knights of Columbus; "public-interest" lobbies like the Naderites or the Sierra Club; but also the widget plant's bowling club and foreman's association, and any number of special pleaders for every conceivable (or inconceivable) cause.

Some service institutions are huge and occupy palaces like the American Association for the Advancement of Science in Washington or the Ford Foundation in New York; others get by with a part-time clerk and an unpaid secretary-treasurer. Some are run and staffed by high-powered professionals, others by volunteers. Some pass the begging bowl; others live off fees; others, like most public libraries and many museums, are supported entirely or in part by tax money.

Beyond what they are not—that is, government agencies or businesses—they seem to have very little in common.

Another reason for our neglect is that their growth has been so very recent. Until, at the most, two decades ago, the service institutions were marginal. Their goals, their performance, their effectiveness, their productivity helped or harmed no one but themselves. By now, however, the Third Sector has become so important, so big, and so costly that we need to focus on how it is being run. Performance, effectiveness, and productivity of the service institutions will increasingly matter. And they will also become increasingly difficult. Precisely because they have grown so much the service institutions require more and better management—and they require different management.

After such explosive growth, yesterday's way of doing things has become inappropriate if not counter-productive. Today's hospital is surely a very different institution from that of seventy-five years ago which existed largely to give the poor a decent place to die, a place, that is, that dispensed "charity." The museum that attracts such crowds that it has to ration access surely serves purposes different from its old role as a "cultural bastion" for the "refinement of the wealthy classes," to quote from a nineteenth-century description. But what are its new purposes? And what should they be?

Largely because the organizations for international student exchange—helped, of course, by the charter plane—have done so good a job, today's middle-class American (and European) youngster takes living and traveling abroad for granted. Do the student-exchange programs still serve a purpose and what is it?

One organization that has faced such questions is CARE. It still handles food parcels, still helps feed people all over the world who are overtaken by disaster—and does the job well, cheaply, and efficiently. But it also has been building on its success and acceptance as a relief agency to become a development agency that challenges poor peasants all over the world to become productive, knowledgeable, and self-supporting agriculturalists.

The success of the evangelical churches may well be based less on conservatism than on their willingness to face up to the fact that in today's overinstitutionalized society the first job of the minister is no longer to be a *social* agency—the job that made the American Protestant church so effective in the early years of the century; it may be to minister to the individual.

But, by and large, few service institutions attempt to think through the changed circumstances in which they operate. Most believe that all that is required is to run harder and to raise more money.

And fewer still are willing to accept that success always means organizing for abandoning what has been achieved. In service institutions abandonment is particularly difficult. They are not *want*-oriented; they are *need*-oriented. By definition they are concerned with good works and with social or moral contributions rather than with returns and results. The social worker will always believe that the very failure of her efforts to get a family off welfare proves that more effort and more money are needed.

Yet precisely because results in service institutions aren't easily measured, there is need for organized abandonment. There is need for systematic withdrawal of resources—money and, above all, people—from yesterday's efforts. The manager of a service institution must constantly ask the unpopular question, "Knowing what we now know, would we get into this activity, this service, this effort if we were not already in it?" And if the answer is "no," he shouldn't ask for another study or try to find a way to repackage the old chestnut to make it look fresh to the donors. He should find a way to get out of that service as quickly as possible. At the very least, he should ask himself how methods should be changed to accomplish what his institution originally set out to accomplish.

Both the businessman and the civil servant tend to underrate the difficulty of managing service institutions. The businessman thinks it's all a matter of being efficient, the civil servant thinks it's all a matter of having the right procedures and controls. Both are wrong—service institutions are more complex than either businesses or government agencies—as we are painfully finding out in our attempts to make the hospital a little more manageable (no one to my knowledge has tried to do this with the university).

Indeed we know far too little about managing the non-profit institution—it is simply too recent a phenomenon. But we do know that it needs to be managed. And we do know that defining what its task is and what it should not be is the most essential step in making the institutions of the Third Sector manageable, managed, and performing.

(1978)

CHAPTER NINETEEN

Managing the Knowledge Worker

DIRECT PRODUCTION WORKERS—machinists, bricklayers, farmers—are a steadily declining portion of the work force in a developed economy. The fastest growing group consists of "knowledge workers"—accountants, engineers, social workers, nurses, computer experts of all kinds, teachers, and researchers. And the fastest growing group among knowledge workers themselves are managers. People who are paid for putting knowledge to work rather than using brawn or manual skill are today the largest single group in the American labor force—and the most expensive one.

The incomes of these people are not, as a rule, determined either by supply or demand or by their productivity. Their wages and fringe benefits go up in step with those of manual direct-production workers. When the machinists get a raise, the foreman's salary goes up by the same percentage more or less automatically—and so does everybody else's in the company right up to the executive office.

But whether the productivity of the knowledge worker goes up is questionable. Is there reason to believe, for instance, that today's schoolteachers are more productive than the teachers of

1900—or today's engineer, research scientist, accountant, or even today's manager?

At the same time the knowledge worker tends to be disgruntled, or at least not fully satisfied. He is being paid extremely well. He does interesting work and work that does not break the body as so much of yesterday's work did. And yet the "alienation" of which we hear so much today (I personally prefer to use the good old word "distemper") is not primarily to be found in the working class. It is above all a phenomenon of the educated middle class of employed knowledge workers.

We do not know how to measure either the productivity or the satisfaction of the knowledge worker. But we do know quite a bit about improving both. Indeed, the two needs—the need of society and economy for productive knowledge workers and the need of the knowledge worker for achievement—while distinctly separate, are by and large satisfied by the same approaches to managing the knowledge worker.

1.

We know first that the key to both the productivity of the knowledge worker and his achievement is to demand responsibility from him or her. All knowledge workers, from the lowliest and youngest to the company's chief executive officer, should be asked at least once a year, "What do you *contribute* that justifies your being on the payroll? What should this company, this hospital, this government agency, this university, hold you accountable for, by way of contributions and results? Do you know what your goals and objectives are? And what do you plan to do to attain them?"

Direction of the knowledge worker toward contribution—rather than toward effort alone—is the first job of anyone who manages knowledge workers. It is rarely even attempted. Often the engineering department finds out, only after it has finished the design, that the product on which it has been working so hard has no future in the marketplace.

2.

But at the same time, knowledge workers must be able to appraise their contributions. It is commonly said that research is "intangible" and incapable even of being appraised. But this is simply untrue.

Wherever a research department truly performs (an exception, alas, rather than the rule), the members sit down with each other and with management once or twice a year and think through two questions: "What have we contributed in the last two or three years that really made a difference to this company?" and "What should we be trying to contribute the next two or three years so as to make a difference?"

The contributions may indeed not always be measurable. How to judge them may be controversial. What, for instance, is a greater contribution: a new biochemical discovery that after five more years of very hard work may lead to the development of a new class of medicinal compounds with superior properties; or the development of a sugar-coated aspirin without great scientific value that will improve the effectiveness of pediatric medicine by making the aspirin more palatable for children while also immediately increasing the company's sales and profits?

But unless knowledge workers are made to think through such questions and to review, appraise, and judge their contributions, they will not direct themselves toward contribution. And they will also feel dissatisfied, nonachieving, and altogether alienated.

3.

Perhaps the most important rule—and the one to which few managements pay much attention—is to enable the knowledge workers to do what they are being paid for. Not to be able to do what one is being paid for invariably quenches whatever motivation there is. Yet salesmen, who are being paid for selling and know it, cannot sell because of the time demands of the paper work imposed on them by management. And in research lab after research lab, highly paid and competent scientists are not allowed to do their work but are instead forced to attend endless meetings to which they cannot contribute and from which they get nothing.

Managers may know the rule. But rarely do they know what they or the company do that impedes knowledge workers and gets in the way of their doing what they are being paid for. There is only one way to find out: Ask the individual knowledge worker (and the knowledge-work team he belongs to), "What do I, as your manager, and what do we in the company's management altogether, do that helps you in doing what you are being paid for? ... What do we do that hampers you? ... Specifically, do we give you the time to do what you are being paid for, the information you need to do it, the tools for the job?"

4.

Knowledge is a high-grade resource. And knowledge workers are expensive. Their placement is therefore a key to their productivity. The first rule is that opportunities have to be staffed with people capable of running with them and of turning them into results. To make knowledge workers productive requires constant attention to what management consulting firms and law firms call "assignment control." One has to know where the people are who are capable of producing results in knowledge work—precisely because results are so very hard to measure.

Effective management of the knowledge worker requires a regular, periodic inventory and ranking of the major opportunities. And then one asks, "Who are the performing people available to us, whether they are researchers or accountants, salesmen or managers, manufacturing engineers or economic analysts? And what are these people assigned to? Are they where the results are? Or are their assignments such that they could not produce real results, no matter how well they perform?"

Unless this is being done, people will be assigned by the demands of the organization—that is by the number of transactions rather than by their importance and their potential of contribution. In no time they will be misassigned. They will be where they cannot be productive, no matter how well-motivated, how highly qualified, how dedicated they are.

One also has to make sure that knowledge workers are placed where their strengths can be productive. There are no universal geniuses, least of all in knowledge work which tends to be highly specialized. What can this particular knowledge worker do? What is he or she doing well? And where, therefore, does he or she truly belong to get the greatest results from his or her strengths?

Most businesses and other organizations as well spend a great deal of time and money on the original employment of people who, it is hoped, will turn into knowledge workers. But at that stage one knows very little about the future employees—beyond the grades they got in school, which have little correlation with future performance capacity. The true personnel management job, in respect to knowledge workers, begins later, when one can place workers where their strengths can be productive because one knows what they can do.

Manual strength is additive. Two oxen will pull almost twice the load one ox can pull. Skill is capable of subdivision. Three men, each of whom has learned one aspect of a skill, e.g., gluing the legs to a table, can turn out far more work of equal skill than one man skilled in all aspects of carpentry. But in knowledge work two mediocre people do not turn out more than one man capable of performance, let alone twice as much. They tend to get in each other's way, and to turn out much less than one capable person. In knowledge work, above all, one therefore has to staff from strength. And this means constant attention to placing knowledge workers where what they can do will produce results and make a contribution.

Knowledge is perhaps the most expensive of all resources. Knowledge workers are far more expensive than even their salaries indicate. Each of them also represents a very sizable capital investment—in schooling and in the apprentice years during which the worker learns rather than contributes (such as the five years which every chief engineer knows will be needed before young graduates can truly be expected to earn their salaries). Young engineers, young accountants, young market researchers represent a "social capital investment" of something like $100,000 to $150,000 each before they start repaying society and their employers through their contributions. No other resource we have is equally "capital intensive" and "labor intensive." And only management can turn the knowledge worker into a productive resource.

But, also, no one expects to achieve, to produce, to contribute quite as much as the knowledge worker does. No one, in other words, is more likely to be alienated if not allowed to achieve.

Not to manage a knowledge worker for productivity therefore creates both the economic stress of inflationary pressures and the highly contagious social disease of distemper. We can indeed measure neither the productivity nor the satisfaction of the knowledge worker. But we know how to enrich both.

(1975)

CHAPTER TWENTY

Meaningful Government Reorganization

DURING HIS 1976 CAMPAIGN Jimmy Carter repeatedly promised to streamline the federal government, to amalgamate its agencies and to create such new "super agencies" as a Federal Department of Energy. In this, he simply followed the precedents set by every one of his predecessors since Franklin D. Roosevelt in his 1936 campaign.

There is indeed need to overhaul the bureaucratic sprawl in Washington. But Mr. Carter's proposals were unlikely to have any more impact on governmental performance than the proposals of his predecessors. Reshuffling the organization chart will not make a single agency more effective or perform better. Even zero-budgeting and zero-revenue planning, the new and far more radical measures proposed to control government spending and taxes, will have only limited impact, desirable and necessary though both approaches are.

If the new President really intends to make government more effective, however, we know what to do. At least we know the first three steps.

1. Require clear and specific goals for every government agency and for each program and project within each agency. What are needed are not just statements of broad policies—these are simply good intentions—but targets with specific timetables and clear assignments of accountability. The budget, of course, tells how much money an agency intends to spend and where. But it rarely tells what results are expected. In other words, budgets are spending plans which make vague promises, but they omit mention of social and economic changes that result from government action.

   So the first step toward better governmental performance is to establish clear targets, targets which specify the expected results and the time necessary to achieve them. Then what is needed is a systematic study and report each year of how well these targets have been achieved.

2. Each agency needs to establish priorities within its targeted objectives, so that it can concentrate its effort. Practically without exception, government agencies lack priorities and steadfastly refuse to set them.

   Every police department in the United States knows that crime on the street is a first priority, which requires concentrating uniformed officers on patrol duty. But few police departments dare say "no" to the old lady who phones in to complain that a cat is caught in a tree in her front yard. Instead, it sends a patrol car. Yet police departments probably have the clearest objectives and the keenest sense of priorities of all our public agencies.

   By contrast, the enormous bureaucracies in such cabinet departments as Health, Education and Welfare (HEW) or in Housing and Urban Development are so badly subdivided among so many aimless programs that, despite their hordes of employees, few programs are staffed adequately to achieve results.

Setting priorities is difficult in politics because every program has its own constituencies. So setting priorities requires a great deal of courage, but this after all is what a chief executive—in the federal government or in a private business—is paid for.

3. Finally, the toughest, most novel, but also the most important prerequisite of organizational effectiveness is organized abandonment.

Political philosophy maintains that the tasks of government are perennial and can never be abandoned. This may have made sense when government confined itself to such basic functions as defense, administration of justice, and domestic order. Those days are long past, of course, yet this is still the way we run government. The underlying assumption should be that everything government does is as likely as every other human activity to become unproductive or obsolete within a short time. To keep such activities going requires infinitely more effort than to run the productive and successful ones.

Political philosophy has also always maintained, although not quite as firmly, that results and performance are not a proper yardstick by which to measure governmental programs. Those measurements belong to economics, which assumes that efforts are being made for the sake of results. But when governmental efforts produce disappointing performance and results it is always agreed that this only indicates that greater effort and more money are needed since "the forces of evil are so powerful."

Antitrusters, for instance, clearly believe that the fewer results their efforts bring, the more effort is deserved; to them, the absence of results does not prove the inappropriateness of the antitrust approach but the overpowering presence of conspiracy and evil. The experience of countries that, with practically no antitrust efforts, have industrial structures not very different from our own does not impress the dedicated antitruster any more than sex statistics from other parts of the world would impress the Puritan thundering from the pulpit against fornication.

But even the most convinced moralist would likely admit that the bulk of governmental efforts today belong in the category of economics, in which results are the proper measurement of an activity and the proper concern of management.

Governmental agencies should therefore be required to abandon one program or one activity before a new one can be started. Lack of any such policy is probably why new efforts over the last twenty years have produced fewer and fewer results. The new programs may well have been necessary and even well-planned, but their execution had to be entrusted to whoever was available rather than to the experienced people stuck in unproductive and obsolete jobs.

A good deal of what goes on in HEW or in the Food and Drug Administration clearly needs to be abolished after the programs have accomplished their objectives. Our present "welfare mess" is, to a very large extent, the result of our having kept alive the successful welfare programs of the Great Depression. When a new welfare problem arose in the 1960s, we slapped on old programs designed for totally different purposes.

Most of the farm programs of the New Deal should be abandoned. Social Security, as it was designed in 1935, belongs here too, I suspect. It has been overtaken by profound changes in American demographics—by the surge of life expectancies and by the rise of employer-financed pension plans. The food-stamp program rapidly became the wrong kind of welfare program, regimenting expenditures of the poor rather than giving them additional purchasing power. Most of our housing subsidies probably belong in the same category.

These are initial steps toward improving government performance. They are by no means enough, but even for them the political obstacles erected by the bureaucracies and vested interests will be tremendous. Still, there is now both popular and legislative support for "sunset laws" which provide for the automatic lapse of governmental agencies and programs. And, as Mr. Carter rightly pointed out during his campaign, the foremost need of modern government is to make government more effective. It may even be a condition necessary for the survival of modern government.

(1977)

CHAPTER TWENTY-ONE

The Decline in Unionization

IN 1945 ALMOST 40 PERCENT of the American labor force was unionized. By 1977 the percentage had fallen to 26 percent. (*1981 note:* And in 1981 it was down to 20 percent or less.)

In 1945 practically the entire union membership was in the private sector, in which unionization approached 50 percent. Since then, the great growth of union membership has been in public-service employment—in government, in hospitals, in schools, and so on.

In the private sector, therefore, at most one of every six employees is a union member and membership is heavily concentrated in mature if not declining industries. (*1981 note:* In the private sector, union membership is now back to where it was before the tremendous unionization wave of the 1930s.)

Union membership in the public sector is still growing. But it is clearly running into increasing resistance from taxpayers and from public service employers. It is doubtful whether the public service unions can hold on to recent gains, especially with respect to job security and retirement pay, considering the severe financial crisis of local governments.

At the same time, membership in traditional private sector unions is changing fast. For instance, the new manual workers are less well educated, as a rule, than the rest of the population and no better educated than the men and women whom they replace—a startling reversal of a long-term American trend.

Young people with schooling go on to college or to a community college, and as a rule are not available for the traditional blue-collar jobs. The ones who are feel themselves to be "losers" before they start and are correspondingly militant. They also have far less allegiance than older members to the union as a "cause."

Union leadership is about to be replaced. Even the "young" men among the traditional leaders are in their sixties. And with the steady decline in relative union strength, together with the steady erosion of leadership, has come a decline in political power (consider labor's startling impotence with the Carter Congress and the Carter Administration, both of whom owed their election to organized labor) and in public esteem (every opinion poll shows the public has less trust in labor than in any other institution).

Given this mistrust, frustration, and labor's sense almost of despair, we can expect very rough times ahead in labor-management relations.

But at the same time the issues are changing. Labor will continue to push for "more," but it will push for "different" as well.

Employment security is clearly an emerging central issue. The steelworkers, in the 1975 round of contract negotiations, made significant advances toward lifetime employment for members. That goal will increasingly become part of the labor movement, in private and public sector employment.

With lifetime employment or some variant thereof, it will be management's responsibility to find new jobs for workers whose existing jobs are being altered or abolished through changes in technology. This will require a kind of manpower planning which, so far, is virtually unknown in American industry (but which has long been commonplace in Japan and in Sweden).

Then there is the issue of union security. Union leaders do not just fight for the jobs of members, they also fight for their own jobs and for the survival of their own organizations.

The new jobs in American industry are not where the traditional unions are. They are not in the mass-production industries. They are not in craftwork, such as the building trades. Therefore, traditional unions see themselves as being elbowed aside and threatened with extinction. This will undoubtedly lead to jurisdictional strife between unions vying with each other for a larger piece of an ever-smaller pie. But it will also lead increasingly to union demands to freeze employment, to freeze technologies, and to freeze jurisdictions.

Perhaps the most difficult and yet the most important issue related to employment security is that caused by the population dynamics of the American labor force. It cannot be said too often that the great majority of people now reaching retirement age are blue-collar workers or low-grade clerks with limited education. A majority of young people entering the labor force have advanced schooling and are therefore not readily available for the traditional jobs on the assembly line, in the cab of a truck, or behind a sales counter.

Add to this the fact that the number of people entering the labor force (other than young blacks) will drop by 30 percent in the early eighties (as a result of the "baby bust" that started in the early 1960s) and we face a severe shortage of replacements for retiring blue-collar and clerical workers.

At the same time, the developing countries now need to find manufacturing jobs and jobs in export industries for the tremendous number of their young people who reach maturity as a result of the population explosion that started in the late 1950s.

So the situation is this: No matter what wage we pay, we will not be able to find enough people to do traditional work and we will have to subcontract labor-intensive work to developing countries. Increasingly, we will have to move toward an international exchange of work by stages of production. But this, of course, threatens the remaining workers in industries at home.

The best example of this is the 50,000 or so shoe workers, mostly elderly and mostly concentrated in a small area, whose jobs are being threatened by imports. Yet we could not possibly find enough labor in this country to produce the shoes we need.

The same is largely true with respect to steel, where labor-intensive American industry has been outflanked by a highly mech-anized steel industry in Japan and by cheap labor in new automated steel industries of the developing world, e.g., Korea.

How is this to be handled if we accept—as we are about to do—the principle of lifetime employment? Protectionism is the obvi-ous answer, but it is clearly the wrong solution. It will not help workers or employers except for a very short time. For protection-ism helps only if an industry is growing. Otherwise, it harms the industry and the economy within a fairly short period.

At the same time, public policy will clearly not remain indiffer-ent to genuine hardship. By and large, the workers who are threat-ened by "production sharing" in the international economy are older men and women not easily retrained or placed in other jobs. Should this be considered a national obligation (the approach taken in the Nixon Administration) or an industry problem (which is how steelworkers and automobile workers see it)? At any rate, it is clearly going to be a major labor-management problem.

Then there are the problems created by the rapid growth of work groups that do not fit any traditional molds: the older worker who has reached what is usually considered retirement age but who continues working now that fixed-age retirement is rapidly disap-pearing. Or the older married women who are joining the labor force in growing numbers and who increasingly need part-time rather than full-time employment. The question of the rights, ben-efits, and obligations of these groups has not been tackled yet. For example, what about their seniority and promotions?

These are all issues that will certainly come up eventually, but for which neither management nor labor is yet prepared. And there are other issues. Among them: indexing of compensation to offset the higher tax bracket into which inflation automatically pushes the employee, substantially reducing his disposable income. And settling the question of union representation on boards of directors and on the governing boards of employee pension funds.

The question is not whether these issues will arrive; they have already. The question is whether management will leave the initiative entirely to labor, as it has done for decades. The answer to that will go a long way toward determining the outcome of tomorrow's labor relations and labor policies.

(1977)

CHAPTER TWENTY-TWO

The Future of Health Care

PRESIDENT CARTER ANNOUNCED in the fall of 1978 "principles" for major health-care legislation. But the future American health-care system is being built right now, and without benefit of legislation. Mr. Carter's proposals, whatever they were, were "nonstarters." There were days of congressional hearings on them with mountains of testimony, studies, and reports. But if these produced anything at all, it was the proverbial *ridiculus mus*, the ridiculous, tiny mouse.

The reason for this is not even resistance to the costs of new government programs. It is the total absence of grassroots pressure for major health-care changes.

It is simply not true that the American people are dissatisfied with the health-care delivery system. The overwhelming majority in any survey—some 90 percent or so—declare themselves "well satisfied" or "highly satisfied." It is even less true that Americans feel themselves "suffering under the staggering costs of a fee-for-service system," as I heard one of our distinguished senators orate recently.

Doctors and hospitals are in large part on a fee-for-service basis; patients are not. Nineteen out of twenty of us—around 95 percent of the population—have a prepayment health plan and do not pay for the services we receive. Indeed, that may be one of the reasons why health-care costs are so hard to control.

The majority of us are enrolled in employment-based plans with the rest being on Medicare or Medicaid. And most of us neither know nor care what our individual health-care insurance costs. It is considered to be "free" in most cases; that is, the costs, as in a national health plan, are being paid through a compulsory levy that is pre-take-home pay and pre-income tax.

The only reason, I suspect, that we still hear of a national health service is Senator Edward Kennedy's—understandable—desire to have his name on one piece of major national legislation. Even the unions who sign their names to the Kennedy proposal and testify for it are at best lukewarm. Every one of the union officers and union staffers with whom I have talked wants health-care benefits to remain a bargainable issue which, of course, it would cease to be if we legislated a national health service that covers everything for everybody.

Indeed, most union leaders—and even more their staff advisers—see health-care benefits as the *only* area of potential union gains in the years ahead, considering the resistance to wage increases and to higher taxes, and freedom to bargain on health-care benefits as essential to the very survival of the American labor movement.

While the politicians fight sham battles, the future American health-care system—at least for 95 percent of the population—is rapidly emerging and can be predicted with very high probability. It will be different from the present one in three aspects: in the coverage of health-care costs; in its pluralism of health-care deliverers; and in its organized control and self-control of medical standards and health-care costs.

Sooner or later around three quarters of the American people will have catastrophic-illness insurance—fewer than 60 percent have it today. Ten years hence 95 percent will have it. There will be no ceiling, that is, no maximum beyond which the insurance does not pay. There is actually no such ceiling today—except in the contract. As every hospital knows, charges not covered by the catastrophic-illness policy are not collectible.

But while the incidence of above-ceiling costs is quite small, the fear of them is real. We might, however, see a good deal of emphasis on a fairly high deductible—a floor for catastrophic-illness reimbursements—and on some coinsurance feature up to a certain amount or to a certain percentage of the insured's family income. And perhaps we will see government reinsurance of catastrophic-illness costs for the 5 percent noninsurables—first proposed thirty years ago by President Eisenhower.

Five years hence two fifths of the population—the employees in large companies and governments—will be insured for the costs of prescription drugs, again with a deductible perhaps of $100 a year per family. More important—and more costly—by 1990 or so around half of the families in America will have insurance for dental bills—and by 1995 the great majority will have it. By then also the expenses for the three most common medical appliances—corrective glasses, hearing aids, and dentures—will be insured for the majority.

The vehicle for these extensions of coverage will not be law but contracts between individual employers and their employees. Emotional problems will not, however, be covered by most of these contracts, I believe, except in the case of genuine psychotic ailments requiring hospitalization. The cost of psychotherapy is much too high and impossible to control. Despite assertions by the "experts" that "three out of four" Americans suffer from emotional illness, the belief in the efficacy of psychotherapy has probably crested and may be going down very fast.

Most of the current discussion of health-care delivery poses a choice between the individual physician practicing alone or the Health Maintenance Organization (HMO), a collective of physicians operating out of one central location and controlling their own hospital. But the American health-care system of tomorrow will consist of three parallel and competing channels of delivery:

the private physician, the Individual Physicians Association (IPA), and the HMO.

The bulk of health-care delivery ten years hence will still be with the private physician, though more and more will have what are (erroneously) called group practices, that is share offices, office staffs, and labs. Next in importance will be the IPA. Employers in certain areas will get together and set standards and fees for medical services, with the help of a medical director or counselor. Physicians who agree to meet the standards and fee levels will be recommended to employees by the IPA.

This is essentially the system that has been working well in Germany for eighty years. It preserves freedom of choice on the part of the patient, but also provides a means of cost and quality control. Such plans already exist in the United States and are growing fast.

The HMO, on the other hand, will grow only to the extent to which government imposes it. I used to be a fervent advocate of HMOs. But it may well be an idea whose time has passed, despite fervent advocates in Washington. The IPA does everything the HMO does but without the latter's limitations—that is, the absence of physician choice and a permanent physician-patient relationship. The only cost advantage of the HMO is its ability to concentrate its patients in one centrally managed health-care facility. But in a decentralized country such as the United States, and with more and more women working miles from their husband and children, this isn't an advantage at all.

The great attraction of an IPA is that policing of standards will stay within the medical fraternity. The IPA director and its medical council will decide which physicians will be admitted to practice for the subscribers.

Peer review of doctors by doctors in hospitals is growing because of malpractice suits and government pressure. Coming even faster is systematic review of hospital costs by Blue Cross and other insurers, as well as by employers and large unions. Ten years hence, large employers, government bodies, IPAs, and hospitals will jointly determine medical standards and costs in typically American fashion—disorderly and decentralized.

It is simply not true that the American health-care system is more expensive than any other—it may actually be among the cheaper ones in terms of gross national income and family income. The figures that are bandied about of the lower costs of other systems are simply phony—the real cost of the British National Health Service, for instance, is not "under 7 percent of GNP"; it is closer to 12 percent, considering that the British have to spend almost as much on making good their shortage of hospital beds as they are spending on current health-care operations and that more and more Britons enroll in private health-insurance plans.

It is simply not true that our health-care costs have risen faster than those of other countries—they have risen much faster in Germany and in Sweden, for instance. It is simply not true that America uses hospitals more than anyone else. In every developed European country, hospital admissions per thousand population are higher than in the United States, hospital stays are longer, and in most of them the per diem cost is higher.

It may not even be true that health-care and especially hospital costs have risen faster than any other major item in America and faster than inflation—that may be true only for those costs, such as Medicaid, that are imposed by government.

In other words, there are good reasons why the great majority of Americans in every survey declares itself as "pretty satisfied" with its health-care system and why there is no grassroots pressure for more than minor changes in it.

(1978)

CHAPTER TWENTY-THREE

The Professor as Featherbedder

WITHOUT MAJOR CHANGES IN POLICY, college and university professors are likely to become an endangered species in the decades ahead—and unionization and political lobbying are unlikely to help any more than they have helped to protect the anthracite coal mines or the railroads.

In their own self-interest, faculty members need radically new policy in three areas. They need an effective substitute for a self-defeating tenure policy. They need systematic personnel development to enable them to benefit from future opportunities. And they need organized placement of the middle-aged, average professor in work and careers outside of academe. But, above all, faculty members need management—either self-imposed management or management by administrators.

The one change in status that professors are likely to resist the most strenuously is any change in the tenure system. But tenure will increasingly become a threat—even to tenured faculty members. Rather than protect professors against change, it will entrap them. Without changes in tenure policy, colleges will soon be unable to bring in new people. That, in turn, can only accelerate the decline in graduate enrollment, thus creating greater pressures to cut both faculty size and faculty salaries. But at the same time, for twenty or more years ahead, college faculties will be aging—and any group unable to renew itself becomes stagnant, stale; ultimately, it putrifies. The present tenure policy condemns higher education to becoming a declining industry and eventually a dying industry. Colleges are likely to become the railroads of the knowledge industry.

Tenure in its present form does not even protect faculty members who possess it. If there is no way to adjust faculty assignments to changes in enrollment and revenue—and this is what present tenure policy implies—then there are only three ways to go.

One is to continue the downward pressure on salaries, and especially on the salaries of the great majority—the merely competent professors of forty-five or fifty. It is self-delusion to believe that political or union pressure on legislatures can even slow the erosion of faculty incomes; there would be mighty little political sympathy for the professor, nor indeed would the professor deserve more than any other featherbedder.

A second way would be for college administrators to close down entire departments and areas of study. A college may have enough students for a fine arts department of three or four faculty members. But if the department has nine professors, all of them tenured, then the only way to adjust is to drop the fine arts department. And if the courts rule that this violates tenure, that tenure gives a right to a job, then we may see the wholesale closing of a number of institutions—and by no means only small ones.

The third way would be to give professors a series of contracts—maybe three-three-five-five-five years, with an automatic extension for one year in case the contract is not renewed, thus giving the faculty member ample time to look around. The decision to grant a contract would have to be made with due process, which would imply not only faculty participation but also outside participation by distinguished and respected members of the faculties of other institutions, and preferably of other disciplines as well, and probably also of laymen, particularly alumni. Only after a person had held five or six contracts—by which time he or she would probably be past fifty—would tenure be in order.

College faculty members also need organized personnel development. They need to prepare themselves for the opportunities ahead. For we can expect to see substantial growth of college enrollments in two areas: in the continuing education, both professional and general, of already highly schooled adults and in the community college. But young academicians today are not encouraged to make themselves employable in respect to these opportunities. Anyone who has worked in continuing-education programs for adults, whether in advanced management programs or in programs in the humanities (and I have done both) knows that the great majority of faculty members, even able ones, cannot do the work, fail, and have to be removed. They do not know how to teach, especially how to teach adults. They are so narrowly specialized as to appear virtually illiterate to mature, experienced men and women. In the community college the ability to relate subject matter to experience, to application, to learning—though at a much lower level—is equally needed.

The system of rewards and incentives in higher education promotes specialization and isolation. Although this may be the right direction today for an individual faculty member at the start, it will increasingly be the wrong direction, considering the opportunities of tomorrow, for his development and employability. To get ahead, to get promoted, to get more pay, the academic will have to be employable where the opportunities will be—that is in advanced and continuing education of adults or in the community college.

There is need, in other words, for systematic development of faculty personnel. There is need for doing in academic life what is now standard practice in all other areas of employment in the knowledge industries: systematic self-development of the professional, in view of his or her own desires and abilities and in view of the needs and opportunities of profession, employer, market, and society. Concretely, this means exposing younger academicians to the challenges of teaching and research work outside of their own specialties; to teaching and research with different kinds of students; and to opportunities for learning, especially for learning a bit about teaching.

If there is no organized self-development of the individual in academe, we are likely to see imposed efficiency and compulsory conformity, as opportunities for employment, advancement, and income change. Instead of looking at individuals and asking, "What are their strengths and desires, their greatest opportunities, their greatest needs?" we may well rush into a standardized training program. It is precisely because the strength of higher education lies in diversity and in individual and highly specific contributions that faculty members need an organized and directed development effort, an effort focused both on the strengths and desires of the individual faculty member and on the opportunities in higher education.

Finally, academe needs organized placement—as much as any other group in the knowledge fields, if not more so. It needs such efforts, above all, for the middle-aged, mid-career faculty member, the man or woman of forty-five whose own self-interest in a great many cases demands placement outside of academe and in other work.

By the time faculty members reach their early or mid-forties, they typically have been in academic life for twenty years—and typically have not worked in any other environment. Most faculty members, by that time, have done all the research and have written all the books they will ever write. Beyond that age only a very small number of first-rate people remain productive. To be sure, these scholars and teachers who continue to produce are the people of whom everybody thinks when talking of historians, anthropologists, or metallurgists—but their number is very small indeed. The rest have, in effect, retired into boredom. They know their stuff, but they are no longer excited by it. They need a different environment, a different challenge, a different career. They need to be "repotted."

This middle-aged faculty member is far from being burned out. But he is bored. And the common remedies—to get a divorce and take up with a nineteen-year-old undergraduate; to take to the bottle; to take to the psychoanalyst's couch—don't cure the disease. And unless this competent but bored person finds a new challenge, a new environment, and different work and different colleagues, irreversible deterioration soon sets in.

Professors need organized placement efforts which find the outside opportunities, whether in government, in industry, or in professional practice, and which help the individual to move to them. And this is also the one best way to restore higher education's ability to attract young people at a time of shrinking enrollments and budgets.

Other professions have long ago recognized that they have to place people. The young lawyers, accountants, or management consultants, no matter how well they perform, will be placed elsewhere by their firm if, around age thirty-five, they do not look like the right people for a partnership, that is if they lack the ability to conduct an assignment for a client or to bring in new clients. Ten years later, senior members of these professional practices look again at their partners and place elsewhere those who are not going to become senior partners. While not a contractual obligation, the placement efforts of the accounting firm or management consulting firm guarantee the associate an attractive job that fits the individual's abilities, needs, and the stage of his or her personal life cycle.

Faculty members have these needs too. Yet such solutions do not fit in easily with the traditional concept of the scholar—whether the German Herr Professor or the English don. But American college and university faculty members today no longer fit those European models. Jobs for 500,000 or so faculty members exist only because higher education has become an employment—a very large employment. But even though higher education has become mass education and big business, we must do the things that will save the essence of the scholar: freedom, self-direction, leadership role. Otherwise, college and university faculty members in twenty years will have become just employees—junior high school teachers with inflated degrees and deflated pay—in their standing, their self-respect, their influence, and their role in society.

(1979)

CHAPTER TWENTY-FOUR

The Schools in 1990

THE BIGGEST INFRASTRUCTURE CHALLENGE for this country in the next decade is not the billions needed for railroads, highways, and energy. It is the American school system, from kindergarten through the Ph.D. program and the postgraduate education of adults. And it requires something far scarcer than money—thinking and risk-taking.

The challenge is not one of expansion. On the contrary, the explosive growth in enrollment over the last thirty years has come to an end. By 1978 more than 93 percent of young people entering the labor force had at least an eighth-grade education. So even if the birth rate should rise somewhat, little expansion is possible for elementary, junior high, and high school enrollments.

Graduate and professional schools are still flush with the last age cohorts of the "baby boom" years. But by 1985 these students will have been succeeded by the leaner age groups of the "baby bust" that began in 1960. Some contraction in enrollments is definitely in store.

The last thirty years of social upheaval in the schools are also over. Busing will continue to be a highly emotional issue in a good many metropolitan areas. And there will still be efforts to use schools to bring women into fields such as engineering that have traditionally been considered male. But this shift has already been accomplished in many fields: Half or more of the accounting students in graduate schools of business, for example, are now women. As for most other social issues, the country will no longer try to use schools to bring about social reform and reconstruction. It's becoming increasingly clear to policy-makers that schools cannot solve all the problems of the larger community.

Instead, the battle cry for the eighties and nineties will be the demand for performance and accountability. For thirty years employers have been hiring graduates for their degrees rather than their capabilities; employment, pay, and often even promotion have depended on one's diploma. Now many major employers are beginning to demand more than the completion of school. Some of the major banks, for example, are studying the possibility of entrance examinations that would test the knowledge and abilities of graduates applying for jobs as management trainees.

Students and parents, too, will demand greater accountability from schools on all levels. Indeed, with teaching jobs remaining scarce, the customers of education—parents, students, school boards—will have the upper hand no matter how militantly teachers unionize. It will be increasingly common to bring lawsuits against school districts and colleges for awarding degrees without imparting the skills that presumably go along with them. And many young people are already switching to practical "hard" subjects. Paying no heed to the incantations of youth culture and the media, they have been shifting from psychology into medicine, from sociology into accounting, and from black studies into computer programing.

Demand for education is actually going up, not down. What is going down, and fairly fast, is demand for traditional education in traditional schools.

Indeed, the fastest-growing industry in America today may be the continuing professional education of highly schooled mid-career adults. Much of it takes place outside the education establishment—through companies, hospitals, and government bureaus that run courses for managerial and professional employees; or through management associations and trade associations. Meanwhile, any number of private entrepreneurs are organizing seminars and courses, producing training films and audio tapes and otherwise taking advantage of growth opportunities that university faculties shy away from.

The demand for continuing education does not take the form that most observers, including this writer, originally expected—namely, "Great Books" classes for adults wanting to learn about the humanities, the arts, the "life of the mind." We face instead an all but insatiable demand for advanced professional education: in engineering and medicine, in accounting and journalism, in law and in administration and management.

Yet the mature adults who come back for such studies also demand what teachers of professional subjects are so rarely able to supply: a humanistic perspective that can integrate advanced professional and technical knowledge into a broader universe of experience and learning. Since these new students also need unconventional hours—evenings, weekends, or high-intensity courses that cram a semester's work into two weeks—their demands for learning pose a vague but real threat to academia. Academia's standard response—producing new Ph.D.s for a new department—is roughly comparable to restyling the buggy whip for leadership in the new market for horseless carriages.

The greatest challenge to educators is likely to come from our new opportunities for diversity. We now have the chance to apply the basic findings of psychological development and educational research over the last hundred years: namely, that no one educational method fits all children.

Almost all youngsters—and apparently oldsters as well—are capable of attaining the same standards within a reasonable period of time. All but a few babies, for instance, learn to walk by the age of two and to talk by the age of three. But no two get there quite the same way, as parents have known for eons.

So too at higher levels. Some children learn best by rote, in structured environments with high certainty and strict discipline. Others thrive in the less-structured permissive atmosphere of a progressive school. Some adults learn out of books, some learn by doing, some learn best by listening. Some students need prescribed daily doses of information; others need challenge, the "broad picture," and a high degree of responsibility for the design of their own work. But for too long, educators have insisted that there is one best way to teach and learn, even though they have disagreed about what the way is.

A century ago, the great majority of Americans lived in communities so small that only one one-room schoolhouse was within walking distance of small children. Then there had to be one right method for everybody to learn.

Today the great majority of schoolchildren in the United States (and all developed countries) live in metropolitan areas with such density that there can easily be three or four elementary schools—as well as junior highs and even high schools—within each child's walking or bicycling distance. There will therefore be increasing demand for some kind of "voucher" system enabling students and their parents to choose between alternative routes to learning offered by competing schools.

Indeed, competition and choice are already beginning to infiltrate the school system. Fundamentalist and evangelical schools and colleges have shown an amazing ability to prosper during a period of rising costs and dropping enrollments elsewhere. All this is anathema, of course, to the public school establishment. But economics, student needs, and our new understanding of how people learn are bound to break the traditional education monopoly just as trucks and airplanes broke the monopoly of the railroads, and computers and "chips" are breaking the telephone monopoly.

In the next ten or fifteen years we will almost certainly see strong pressures to make schools responsible for thinking through what kind of learning methods are appropriate for each child. We will almost certainly see tremendous pressure, from parents and students alike, for result-focused education and for accountability in meeting objectives set for individual students. The continuing professional education of highly educated mid-career adults will become a third tier in addition to undergraduate and professional or graduate work. Above all, attention will shift back to schools and education as the central capital investment and infrastructure of a "knowledge society."

(1981)

PART IV

People at Work

Human nature has not changed much over recorded history. But the skills and the knowledge of people, their work and their jobs, their expectations—and also their life spans and their health—do change, and can change very rapidly. In no area, not even in technology, have the changes of the last thirty years been greater than in the work force; and in no area will the changes be greater—or come faster—in the remaining years of this century than in the work force—its composition, its working habits, its working life.

The phrase "people are our only resource" has been a management slogan for at least eighty years. But far too few executives really look at this resource. The Japanese were among the few exceptions after their defeat in World War II, and this is a major secret of their current success. Executives, by and large, tend to see in their mind's eye labor—that is, the work force of 1920 on Henry Ford's assembly line—rather than the knowledge worker of today. When they say "worker" they tend to see a male adult, aged twenty to sixty-five, working on the machine and employed full-time in a permanent job. Yet more than half of the American labor force today consists of women and of people past sixty-five, a good many of them working part-time or intermittently. And the proportion of the labor force working as machine operators will, in all developed countries, fall below 10 percent by the end of this century.

Altogether, we have moved to an employee society. Eighty or 90 percent of national income is paid out as wage and salary in all developed countries. Directly—through pension funds, for example—or indirectly, employees are fast becoming the main owners and the decisive source of capital. And the job, rather than ownership of land, has already become the true "ownership of the means of production."

CHAPTER TWENTY-FIVE

Unmaking the Nineteenth Century

WE ARE BUSILY ENGAGED in unmaking the two proudest social achievements of the nineteenth-century reformer: that married women do not go out to work but stay at home and are free to devote themselves to family and children, and that older people retire.

Historically, the labor-force participation of women was always equal to that of men—both worked from the time they were able to do so until they dropped. Neither farm nor craftsman's shop can be run alone by either man or woman; both require a couple. And, until recently, all but a minuscule fraction of the human race made its living on the farm or in the craftsman's shop. As late as the mid-nineteenth century—when Dickens wrote his harrowing novel of industrial England, *Hard Times* (published in 1854)—it was only Utopian hope that someday in the remote future married women would not have to leave their children to go out to work. By 1914 it had become the mark of the "self-respecting working man" that "his woman" need not work for wages. And by 1950—only thirty years ago—it had become almost axiomatic that women, excepting only a mere handful at either extreme of the economic scale, would stop working with marriage and surely when the first child was about to arrive. In fact, until thirty—or maybe only twenty—years ago, freeing women from the necessity of taking a paid job was the "progressive" demand and very largely what was meant by "female emancipation." And there was no cause on which liberals, progressives, socialists, and reformers of all stripes agreed as wholeheartedly as the need for laws to protect women by keeping them out of "hazardous" and "demeaning" work and occupations. It was still, for instance, one of Eleanor Roosevelt's great causes.

Now, needless to say, all this is reactionary and discrimination. And for women under fifty the labor-force participation rate is already equal to that of men, regardless of their marital status and almost regardless of their having or not having children.

Mandatory retirement of older people was similarly the "progressive cause" only thirty years ago, and the great "reform achievement." In the past, there were no retired people—for the simple reason that old people, ready for retirement, did not exist in any numbers. The first reliable census of modern times—the 1591 population count in the Adriatic port city of Zara—found 365 people over fifty in a population of 13,441—one out of every forty; there was apparently not one inhabitant older than sixty, let alone anyone over sixty-five. Yet Zara was famous for its salubrious climate and for the longevity of its rugged Dalmatian stock (still one of the longest-lived population groups in Europe). Conditions had hardly changed 250 years later. The plot of one of the most popular Victorian novels, Anthony Trollope's *The Warden* (published in 1851), revolves around the inability of an old-age home in an English Cathedral town to find men older than sixty and thus qualified to become pensioners. When life expectancies began to rise rapidly in the second half of the last century, the support of survivors who were too old to work then became the progressive cause; and retirement became the great social achievement, culminating in the mandatory retirement at sixty-five called for by America's Social Security enacted in 1935 and of the employer-sponsored pension plans that began to proliferate around 1950. But by now retiring for age is discrimination—it is outlawed altogether in California and for federal government employees, and nationwide for almost anyone else until age seventy; there is little doubt that mandatory retirement at any age will soon be a thing of the past throughout the United States.

But the laws limp well behind reality—a very large number of those officially retired do work—only they know better than to tell Uncle Sam about it. For the effective tax rate on the earnings from work between $5,000 and $20,000 a year for people aged between sixty-five and seventy-two is from 80 to 100 percent (a loss of fifty cents in Social Security benefits for every dollar earned up to $20,000, or an effective 50 percent tax; full charge for Social Security contributions—around 7 percent for the employee alone—up to earnings of $25,000; full income tax averaging around 20 percent for the older married couple earning $15,000 a year; and for those working for larger organizations usually another 8 to 10 percent for compulsory health insurance and another 8 to 10 percent for contributions to a pension plan, neither of which much benefits older people). No wonder that being retired is coming to mean getting paid by a former employer for not working and by a new employer for working—and not telling Social Security or Internal Revenue about it. How much moonlighting goes on, we do not precisely know. But estimates of hours worked but not reported run as high as one in every ten—and the largest number of moonlighting hours are being worked by people who are officially retired.

Some reasons for this startling shift are clear. Age sixty-five, the mandatory retirement age of 1919—when we first established it— and of 1935 and the start of Social Security, has been overtaken by life expectancies, by improved health and by greatly improved ability to function despite impairments, and—equally important—by drastic changes in the physical demands made by jobs, so that what was age sixty-five in 1935 corresponds to age seventy-four or seventy-five today. Economic needs, e.g., the pressure of inflation on the fixed incomes of retired people, also play a large part even though Social Security payments are more fully indexed against inflation than any other income excepting only federal employee salaries. But surely, both in respect to the labor-force participation of women and to that of the older, officially retired people, wanting to work rather than to be idle, wanting company stimulus and independence are as important as economics, and may well be more important. Among the older people in particular, one of the main motives is the desire to be independent and not have to live with one's children—rather than being afraid of being maltreated by the young as popular rhetoric has it, the old folks try to escape "togetherness" and "care" and enjoy "benign neglect" as long as they possibly can.

But while we have almost unmade the great social achievements of the last century, we are not returning to the conditions of earlier preindustrial times. Historically, women, while always sharing fully in work, have never done the same tasks as men. On the farm and in the craftsman's shop the sexes were fully equal, but they performed different tasks and rarely worked together. Spinning has everywhere been woman's work; a "spinster" is never male. But weaving and dying were always, and exclusively, tasks for men. On the islands of Polynesia men built the ships, manned them, and did the fishing; women tilled the fields and grew the yams. Throughout the Old World only women milk cows; in the New World only men do so—why, no one knows. And except for the mythical Amazons, women never took part in organized warfare—even the female nurse entered the military only in the late nineteenth century. But can there really be much doubt that in the next war women will take part—perhaps even in combat and next to men?

Historically, men have worked together and women have worked together—but in work the sexes stayed apart. What we are doing now in all areas thus represents an unprecedented social experiment—surely one of the most interesting ones in social history. We are committed to it—but how such experiments work out one does not really know for quite some time—generations rather than decades.

Similarly, in history people worked full-time as long as they possibly could—and often well beyond. Now the old line between working and idleness or nonwork is becoming fuzzy. A good many of the working women work part-time; a large number even work full-time for a period and then "take time out," for a baby, for instance, only to come back into the labor force again, part-time or full-time. There is as little precedent in social history for the working patterns of older people as there is for men and women sharing the same tasks. There is now "control of one's working life"—early retirement followed by a return to work, full-time or part-time; these are "second careers"—made both possible and necessary by the tremendous lengthening of working-life span from twenty-five years or less a century ago to fifty years now; there is "volunteer work"—for the older person whose financial needs are covered by his or her pension, and so on. For both women and older people of either sex there is increasingly a choice of patterns combining work and nonwork, permanent jobs and casual jobs, paid work and volunteer work. And these two groups together already constitute more than half of all the people in the American labor force, even though in our mind's eye we still assume that a worker is a male adult under sixty-five working full-time. Not all of the women and the older people want to work even when they do, and not all of them want not to work even when they don't. But a very large proportion—probably a good majority—want *some* work; and increasingly, especially among the older people, they want to be able to make the decision for themselves.

Employers, union leaders, politicians—even, *mirabile dictu*, those slow learners, the economists—are beginning to wake up to the impacts of these shifts in employment, working-life patterns, working hours, and benefits. One no longer shocks executives by telling them that they need to structure full-time jobs to be permanently staffed by part-time people. Ten, even five, years ago, benefit options in the place of uniform benefit plans imposed on all employees regardless of age, sex, marital status, and family situation were unheard of. They are becoming commonplace, though organized labor still frowns on them. Marketers everywhere, whether in business or in the hospital, are beginning to adjust to the fact that these developments in the labor force also cause pronounced shifts in market segmentation, in demand, in consumption, and in buying patterns.

But what are the social and political implications? What does it mean, for instance, that the "progressive causes" of yesterday are today's "hang-ups of reactionary pigs" and "discrimination"? Can other "sacred causes" of the "progressives" and "reformers" of yesterday—or of today—similarly be expected to become "reactionary hang-ups" and "discrimination" tomorrow—as a result perhaps of the same demographic changes that have made the staying of women at home and out of the work force and the mandatory retirement of the elderly into "symbols of oppression"? It is quite conceivable that we are in for a period of very rapid change in which yesterday's "liberal heroes" become the "rearguard of reaction" overnight—the way, perhaps, in which yesterday's "progressive unionist" is rapidly becoming Mr. Reagan's "hard-hat" core supporter.

What will the impact be on the family and on the role and place of the American child in the American home and the American school? The "bourgeois family" in which Mom stays at home with the kids has been one of the favorite topics of sociologists, philosophers, politicians, and preachers since before the turn of the century. Depending on one's politics, it was either the "bastion of civilization" or "total alienation which divorces women from reality." Only ten years ago Herbert Marcuse, the philosophical guru of the student rebellion, still trumpeted this old theme that was first played by Flaubert, Karl Marx, and Ibsen. The kids today are fully as much "alienated from reality," that is, kept out of the world of adult work as they were in the "bourgeois family." But Mom—and even

Grandma—knows as much about the world of work as Daddy knows, is fully as much a part of it, familiar with it, conversant with it. How much longer will TV comedies feature the little woman who cannot balance her checkbook when more than half of all students in accounting courses are female? And what will the family of tomorrow look like—not only with two incomes but with two parallel and separate careers, that is with "competitive coexistence"? I don't know whether it will be better or worse than the "bourgeois family"—but it will surely be different.

Finally: What of all that wondrous talk of the "disappearance of the work ethic"? In the very years in which every attitude survey showed that the "work ethic" is gone, both total labor force and the proportion of the population actively in it and at work have risen spectacularly, while the obstacles to labor-force participation of both older men and women have been steadily dynamited out of the way. One lesson of this is an old one: In a good many social matters "attitudes" are secondary and "attitude surveys" a snare and a delusion; what matters is what people do and not what they say they will do, with the correlation anything but predictable. But more important: In retrospect it appears that the last hundred years—the hundred years in which nonworking for married women and older people were the "progressive causes"—were really the years in which the "work ethic" was being undermined. The last twenty years have seen it return with a vengeance.

(1981)

CHAPTER TWENTY-SIX

Retirement Policy

COMPULSORY RETIREMENT AT AGE sixty-five is as good as dead. The only question now is how fast it will be abolished, and all signs point to its going much faster than anyone would have thought likely.

Labor is almost solidly opposed to any change, and business and government have serious misgivings. Yet a bill to outlaw mandatory retirement at any age by nongovernmental employers—even if written into the union contract—was passed in 1977 by both houses of the California legislature. And a parallel bill for government employees was passed shortly thereafter, together with a bill to raise the mandatory retirement age nationally for all other employees to seventy.

The age-sixty-five cutoff long ago became an anachronism. It was first picked in Bismarck's Germany almost a century ago, and then introduced into this country at the time of World War I. It corresponds in terms of today's life and health expectancies to age seventy-four or seventy-five.

Fixed-age retirement at sixty-five therefore throws a great many perfectly healthy and vigorous people on the scrap heap. That they would revolt was certain; and now they have the numbers to succeed, with 10 percent of the population (almost 20 percent of adult population) being sixty-five or older.

But the fixed retirement age of sixty-five was also becoming an untenable burden for Social Security and employer retirement plans.

When Social Security was first adopted in this country in 1935, there were nine to ten adult Americans in the labor force for every male and female over sixty-five. In 1977 the ratio was three to one. By the early 1980s it had reached 2.5 to one.

If we had continued with fixed retirement at age sixty-five, 40 percent of every employee's wage and salary would have to be used to support older people on retirement. Before the end of this century the figure would have been 50 percent. This is far too high to be politically bearable. And it would also build into the economy continuing pressure for higher money wages to maintain real wages and purchasing power.

The argument for removing or raising the fixed retirement age is even more cogent in terms of labor supply and labor economics. Of every 100 people in the labor force who reach sixty-five, eighty or so are blue-collar workers with a high school education or less.

Of every one hundred young people entering the labor force, at least fifty have had advanced education and are simply not available for the traditional jobs in manufacturing, in mining, in transportation, or in service industries.

Except perhaps in the event of a truly catastrophic depression, labor supply for the traditional blue-collar jobs will increasingly be inadequate even if present blue-collar workers are willing to stay on the job beyond age sixty-five.

But while changing or abolishing any fixed retirement age is politically and economically inescapable, the change will create very real problems. Unless handled intelligently, it may impose high additional costs on the economy and leave us with even greater rigidities in terms of employment and individual mobility.

And it may cause serious labor troubles. For example, the employer will have to develop guidelines to determine when employees reach the point where they become incapable of discharging their jobs, and where therefore they must accept compulsory retirement.

We will have to consider what incentives we need to encourage people, especially blue-collar workers, to postpone retirement. We already increase the amount that a beneficiary receives from Social Security with every year he or she stays on the job. Similar incentives, although probably much greater ones, will be needed for private pension plans.

But postponed retirement age will not save Social Security. All we can hope is to prevent further deterioration, to hold the ratio between people at work and people on retirement pension to three to one—or at best to bring it back to where it was ten years ago, to 2.75 to one.

What should be the employment rights and benefits of people who postpone retirement? Should they continue to have seniority when there are major layoffs, even though they can retire on an adequate pension? Or should we try to adopt the Japanese policy, which considers people who stay on the same job after they have reached the age at which they can retire as "temporary employees" who no longer have job security?

These employees should not, I believe, be considered to have seniority rights for promotions and job openings, nor do they in Japan. But should they continue to contribute to the pension plan and Social Security when they do not benefit from additional contributions?

And how should their health insurance be geared in with Medicare? Under most collective bargaining agreements, the employer has to continue to pay full health-insurance costs for these people, even though their hospital and medical costs are adequately covered by Medicare and even though most of these people today pay the Medicare premium for doctors' bills. Here, clearly, is need for substantial change.

A large number of people who take early retirement soon find out that all they wanted was a long vacation. Today these people cannot go back to their original employment. It seems intelligent to provide retirement plans that give people an option, perhaps for the first six months, to return to their jobs. But should they be treated as new employees in terms of seniority, promotion rights, benefits, and, above all, their pensions? Or should they be reinstated with the appropriate actuarial adjustments?

Finally, abolishing fixed-age retirement creates distinct problems for management and professional employees. Here we face no labor shortage—on the contrary, we will have a substantial supply for many years to come. But here also, being fit physically and mentally is often not enough. In those positions there is also need to be "challenged." It is in these groups that we find the most middle-aged people who have retired "on the job" and wait out their pensions.

We can no longer carry these people in the expectation that they will reach age sixty-five soon and retire; these people are likely to stay on after that. We will have to work systematically on their placement in second careers. Without such organized and systematic efforts, abolishing the fixed retirement age will become a serious problem among managerial and professional employees.

Whether we abolish fixed-age retirement altogether or are content for the time being to raise retirement age, we face a change as traumatic as the one which the coming of mass unionism ushered in forty years ago. Labor and management are whistling in the dark, telling each other that few people will want to stay beyond age sixty-five. Both economics and considerations of the "quality of life" for older people strongly argue that a very large minority—and perhaps even a very large majority—will want to keep on working if only part-time for quite a few years beyond the present cutoff age. Two thirds of all Americans age sixty-five or over did work in 1910, after all.

But even if only a minority chooses to stay on until after sixty-five, the implications are so serious that management, labor, and government better start thinking about them. Especially, they should accept the fact that tomorrow, life—or work—will begin at sixty-five.

(1977)

CHAPTER TWENTY-SEVEN

Report on the Class of '68

THE CLASS OF '68—the class of the Vietnam demonstrations on campus and of the street battles at the Chicago Democratic Convention—was the most antibusiness class in America's history and the most radical of all student generations. Right?

"Yes—but ..." The class of '68 has also turned into the most probusiness class among college generations in many decades.

It is the class that went into business careers more heavily than most of its predecessors, if only because job openings in government and education began to disappear as this class reached the job market. It is this class that marked the sharp upturn in MBA degrees which we have seen in the last decade. And it is the class of '68 that has been more successful in business careers than any of its predecessors since the much smaller classes of the 1920s.

With the class of '68, the first babies of the "baby boom" reached maturity. And they came on the heels of the very small birth cohorts of the thirties and forties, so that they entered what was almost a vacuum. As a result, the graduates of '68, barely thirty or thirty-one years old in 1978 (*1981 note:* and not yet middle-aged in 1981) already are moving into leadership positions as assistant vice presidents and assistant treasurers and directors of corporate planning and directors of market research.

They are not yet by and large, in the decision-making jobs (*1981 note:* but now they are getting into them). But when I sit down with the "decision-makers" in my client companies, large or small, we frequently are joined by a member of the class of '68, or at least a graduate of approximately that era. "Meet Johnny Jones, our assistant vice president, data processing," the "big boss" will say. And it is Johnny Jones who has done the homework, who has worked out the agenda, who writes the report afterward, and who then drafts the policy directive for the "decision-maker's" signature. Increasingly, it is not Johnny Jones but Jane Jones. For the class of '68 was the first class with women in significant numbers going into business as management trainees rather than as secretaries.

I cannot claim to have made a scientific study. And I admit that my sample is totally unrepresentative. But the young people whom I see in client organizations and, above all, in businesses—the young people who are now moving into these positions just below the top, where they begin to have real impact and influence—seem to have many traits in common. Moreover, they are different, different from what one would expect from the class of '68, but different also from the middle-aged people from whom they are rapidly taking over.

Contrary to what one would expect, very few—at least among the ones I see in businesses, in hospitals, or in law offices—are in the "soft" areas in business, in personnel, for instance; or in human relations; in environmental affairs; in social responsibility, or even in public relations.

They tend to cluster in the "hard" areas in finance, in accounting, in data processing, in planning, in economic analysis, in market research, and product management. When they come to my office for a day of consulting work, the first thing they put on the table in my conference room is the pocket calculator. They are the first generation for whom the computer is a household pet—neither a threat nor a scientific marvel but a daily tool.

They are not conservatives by such traditional criteria as attitudes on matters of race, creed, or sex. By those yardsticks they are flaming liberals. But they are not liberal in their attitudes toward government and government programs. There they are ultraconservative cynics. They are not isolationists. They are well-traveled and think nothing of taking their vacations cycling through Scotland. But they are not internationalists of the fifties. The Vietnam scars are still raw and bleeding. And development of underdeveloped countries is not a challenge to them.

These young executives of the class of '68 have very different attitudes toward their careers from those anyone expected of them when they rioted against the "system" ten years ago. They tend to be workaholics. They are excited by their work and expect it to be challenging and demanding. There are very few dropouts among them.

They are, at the same time, intensely ambitious to the point of being pushy. They feel that they have to get to the top very fast if they are going to make it at all. For they feel themselves to be pushed from behind. They are conscious of the fact that the age cohorts behind them are even larger, and will continue to be very large for another twelve years or so, until the babies of the "baby boom" are being succeeded by the babies of the "baby bust" that started in 1960. "You have to be near the top by the time you are thirty-five or you'll be trampled under," several of them—men and women—have said to me within the last year when discussing their career expectations.

At the same time, they are definitely not organization men or organization women. They look upon the organization that employs them as their tool. "I think I should stay at my present bank another three years," one of them said to me when he called me up to tell me that he had been given the vice presidency he was bucking for. "But then I will have gotten as far in commercial banking as I can go; and then I think I should shift into a business and into economic analysis or planning."

This careful thinking about their own careers is quite typical. There also is a good deal of what can only be called cynicism, though the class of '68 would call it realism, about inflation and its consequences, about taxes—and tax shelters—and above all about salaries. "We have learned," a young woman in this group said to me, "always to take a raise in lieu of a promotion, but never to take a promotion in lieu of a raise. If they don't pay you more money, it isn't a promotion."

But the greatest difference between the class of '68 and their predecessors is in the attitudes toward management. They expect, indeed they demand, high competence from the boss and genuinely professional management from him. They expect that the organization that employs them actually plans and then carries out its plan. They expect it to have a systematic process for making decisions. They expect it to have a rational personnel policy, which includes, for instance, regular and thorough performance reviews.

They expect, in other words, that management be rational and that managers—and, above all, their own bosses in top management—be professional. They are very critical indeed of the management they see, sometimes hypercritical. Not having much experience themselves, they do not perhaps adequately value experience. They value, perhaps overvalue, system and method and plan.

Off the job, a good many of them are "into consciousness raising" and practice TM or attend est seminars. But on the job they expect, indeed demand, professional, systematic, maybe somewhat humorless management. Their main complaint about the "boss"—a complaint every one of them I have met these last three years has voiced, one way or another—is not that the boss is "an old fogey," "reactionary," or "stupid"—the complaints of young people before them. It is that the boss does not practice the management he preaches.

(1978)

CHAPTER TWENTY-EIGHT

Meaningful Unemployment Figures

THOUGH MOSTLY EMPTY GESTURES, the final version of the Humphrey-Hawkins Full Employment Bill—passed by the Congress in mid-October of 1975 and promising simultaneous reduction of unemployment to 4 percent and of inflation to 3 percent by 1983, a balanced budget, a trade surplus, and, for good measure, higher farm subsidies—still contained one bit of serious mischief. It committed the United States to the traditional unemployment index.

For years it had been known to everyone dealing with economic statistics that this measurement, as it came down to us from the Great Depression, had become meaningless and misleading. The most its few remaining defenders still claimed is that it measures with considerable lack of reliability the number of people in the labor force of this country who, if the pay were right and the hours were right, might be available for at least a little work once in a while. For years a task force of economists and statisticians had therefore been at work in the Department of Labor to develop a new unemployment index.

It would have been politically difficult, in any event, to get such a new index accepted; any change would have meant lowering both the official unemployment count and the definition of "full employ-ment," and would thus have been fought bitterly by Labor. But Humphrey-Hawkins, while fatuous as a "full-employment bill," made sacred cows out of the wrong unemployment index and of an equally wrong, and meaningless, full-employment definition.

The figures which we need to factor employment and unem-ployment into its decisions are, however, available and are indeed printed in practically every newspaper every month. Yet few read-ers, in my experience, know and use the figures properly.

There are three such figures.

1.

The most important and most meaningful one is the number and proportion of people in this country who have jobs. Total employ-ment is far more important than any unemployment figure. As long as both the number of people with jobs and the percentage of the labor force with jobs go up, consumer spending is bound to rise. If both go down significantly over any period of time—three months or more—consumer spending will drop. And if the two diverge, businessmen should be alert for abrupt changes in the labor supply.

Failure to watch the employment rate accounts for many of the serious business mistakes I have seen in the past few years. As most people know by now, both the number of people with jobs and the percentage employed stand at an all-time high, without precedent in the economic history of the United States or, indeed, of any other major country. And this rapid growth took place in years which many economists, using the official employment figures, characterized as "the most serious recession since the Great Depression."

Actually, both the number of people employed and the percent-age of people in employment went down in only three quarters of the six years 1972–78, and then only by the merest flicker. In terms of consumer demand and consumer buying there was, in other words, no recession at all. But a great many consumer-goods and service businesses, seeing only the meaningless but official unemployment figures, completely missed this and, as a result, lost sales and market standing. Even some very big and very well-managed companies have suffered substantial and perhaps permanent damage because they watched the official unemployment figures and thus acted on the assumption of a "severe recession."

2.

The second figure to watch is the employment and unemployment rate for adult male heads of household. It stood in 1978 around 2.75 percent, which, in effect, means severe labor shortages and very strong inflationary wage pressures. Only in a few bad months of the 1975–1977 recession did it reach true unemployment levels of 6 to 7 percent and only for very short periods.

Unemployment among male adult heads of households is what the official unemployment figure was originally designed to measure, way back in the thirties. Then male adult heads of household *were* the American labor force. It is not surprising, therefore, that so many people assume that the official unemployment figure still refers to male adult heads of household. It is this assumption on which most economists base their "full employment" budget or the projection of the alleged "income loss" to the country because of unemployment.

It is also this assumption that made Humphrey-Hawkins put the "full employment" level at 4 percent unemployment. Four percent unemployment for male heads of household is indeed full employment in the United States—anything above it is genuine unemployment and anything below it is labor shortage. The economists' "Phillips Curve," which attempts to measure the trade-off between inflation and unemployment, also swings from deflationary unemployment into excessive and inflationary labor shortage at around the 4 percent unemployment rate for male adult heads of household. And the unemployment rate for male adult heads of household has been a more reliable indicator of inflationary pressures than even Wall Street's darling, the money supply.

But of course our official figure no longer focuses on male adult heads of household. They now constitute no more than two fifths of our labor force. The other three fifths are women, the great majority not "heads of household" but "dependents" holding "second jobs," if not available only for part-time work; people who are officially "retired" but available for part-time work up to the income level at which their earnings endanger their Social Security pension; a good many young adults, not yet burdened with family responsibilities, who optimize their incomes by alternating between periods of full-time employment and periods of official "unemployment," when they draw tax-free unemployment compensation; unemployables registered for "employment" to be eligible for welfare checks and food stamps; and, finally, a sizable number of full-time students, available for part-time work only and then often for no more than an occasional hour or so on a weekend or evening.

Still, adult male heads of household, while only 40 percent of the labor force, account for some two thirds of all hours worked precisely because they are primarily full-time workers. And they account for the overwhelming majority of skilled workers, managers, and professionals.

3.

The last figure to look at is the one the newspapers print first: the official unemployment figure. Statistically, it is an abomination, an *Alice in Wonderland* stew of apples, oranges, and red herrings. Nothing can make it valid again. Economically, it is meaningless. A good many people have been trying to make it again a meaningful economic figure by moving the "full employment" benchmark of the official figures from the traditional 3 or 4 percent up to 6 or 7 percent. While more realistic, this still would not make the figure useful and meaningful for any economic purpose—whether forecasting or economic policy.

And yet *politically*, the traditional unemployment figure is potent. The official figure dominates official rhetoric and thus induces political gestures which, while futile, are likely to be expensive, inflationary, and the more damaging the less actual results they produce. As a measurement of political pressure, the official employment figure is therefore to be taken seriously.

Even if we could get rid of the official unemployment measurement—and Humphrey-Hawkins made this unlikely, for many years—the American labor force has probably become too heterogeneous for employment and unemployment to be measured by any one yardstick. The one measurement that might be valid would, at the same time, be both exceedingly complicated and politically unacceptable. It would convert the number of people available and looking for work into equivalent full-time jobs—the way universities convert part-time and evening students into "full-time equivalents."

Even then, the figure would have to be adjusted for the number of people (largely young whites) who are registered as unemployed only because it optimizes their income; for those who register for work only to obtain welfare benefits; and for the fairly large number of young people (especially blacks) who are kept out of the labor force by the minimum wage laws.

Such a full-time equivalent measure would probably show today (i.e., October 1978) an unemployment rate of around 3.5 percent compared to the official rate of about 6 percent. But pending the development of an index that reflects the heterogeneity of the American labor force, the businessman—and economist and policy-maker as well—would be well advised to steer by at least two and preferably three separate employment indices: the number and proportion of people in the labor force who have jobs; the employment and unemployment figure for male adult heads of households; and the unemployment fiction of the traditional index.

(1978)

CHAPTER TWENTY-NINE

Baby-Boom Problems

THERE HAVE BEEN REPORTS recently that several management consulting firms are offering starting salaries of up to $60,000 a year to top MBA graduates of prestige business schools. Pity the suckers who swallow such bait. Five years hence many are quite likely to find themselves frustrated, defeated, and embittered. And they may then be lucky to find a $30,000 job by way of promotion.

Fancy starting salaries may be tempting to the young graduate and seem like a good way for the firm to gain attention for itself. They may even be justified in some cases. But more than ever the job applicant and the employer need to be taking a close look at what is really being offered.

The class of 1979 wasn't the last class of the "baby boom" years to reach adulthood. Five more such classes are still ahead of us. But the class of '79 may have been the first one to find that the bases ahead of them were loaded.

The very early birth cohorts of the baby boom were thirty years old in 1979. They are assistant vice presidents or even vice presidents in big banks and large companies; associate professors and high school principals in the field of education; deputy administrators in hospitals or public agencies. But they are also, in many cases, at or close to their terminal jobs. The newcomers, the baby cohorts born in the late 1950s and now entering the executive training process, may find that every rung on the ladder ahead of them is occupied.

Earlier baby boom cohorts had it different. They entered the job market when the executive groups in most fields were getting to be overaged. They also reached adulthood at a time when the economy was expanding rapidly. The result was that they were sucked into high positions at a fast clip.

It used to take twenty-five years in a respectable bank to become assistant vice president; in the late sixties and early seventies one reached that position in three or four years. Similarly, it used to take twenty years in a major university to reach full professor; in the sixties and early seventies it often took only five or ten. When I joined the faculty of a major business school in 1949 I was, at age forty, the "baby" of the faculty and the youngest full professor. When I left twenty-two years later, in 1971, the place was full of able and accomplished teachers with full tenure in their late twenties and early thirties.

But the same demographics that made for fast progress in earlier years are going to slow down the ones now entering the job market. The path to rapid advancement will be blocked by people who are just as well educated but only a little older—people who will be on the job for another twenty-five to thirty-five years.

For the ones now entering the executive job market—the ones who are being offered high salaries—there is thus a huge and widening gap between their expectations and the reality they will encounter. What they expect, quite understandably, is modeled after the experience of their older brothers, sisters, and cousins. After all, they are at least as well educated, just as ambitious, just as bright and eager. It's not their fault they were born five years later.

There is need for them to realize that they will have to take control of their own careers far more carefully than their older brothers and sisters. There will be little room for error. They will have to think through at each stage where they really belong; where their strengths can produce results and will be recognized and rewarded; where their temperaments best fit.

Above all, they will have to accept that only continued self-development and advanced education can make them stand out—and they will be lost in the ruck unless they make themselves stand out.

The challenge may be greater for the employers. I am not sure that it still makes much sense to do intensive college recruiting—there is a good deal to be said (especially for the smaller company) in favor of looking for slightly older (and sadly disenchanted) people available for their second job. But surely employers will have to change drastically what they now promise the graduate. They won't be able to deliver the rapid promotion they are still holding out as bait.

More important—and more difficult—they will have to restructure jobs for the young. In the last twenty years we have tended to make entrance jobs smaller and smaller and less demanding; we had to get young people ready for promotions fast. Now we will have to structure jobs on the assumption that even a capable and hard-working person may have to spend many years on or near the entrance level. Early assignments will have to be made more demanding and more challenging; the ambitious young person must have an opportunity to achieve—or to fail.

In the last fifteen years the main emphasis in many organizations has not been on the job at all but on promotions: When will the new employee be ready to move up? This was shortsighted even when promotions were plentiful; even then, most employees weren't moving up. Promotions have always been the exception and now the emphasis will be back where it belongs: on the job. This will mean drastic changes in incentives, appraisals, job structure, and manager development.

But, above all, there is need to counsel the young. There is need to make sure they have someone to whom they can talk in the organization, if only to unburden themselves. There is need of someone who is concerned with the problem of the young getting to the place in the organization—or outside the organization, for that matter—where their strengths are most likely to be productive and recognized.

There is need for someone who realizes that the young, through no fault of their own or ours, are going to have it tough in the coming years.

(1979)

CHAPTER THIRTY

Planning for Redundant Workers

THE PLIGHT OF CHRYSLER will create a new demand for redundancy planning—that is, anticipating structural and technological changes in the economy and preparing to retain and find new jobs for workers who will have to be laid off.

During the next few years this demand will be intensified by the almost predictable closing of a number of steel mills that will become technically obsolete beyond repair. Indeed, labor unions are already proposing that Congress impose redundancy planning on industry.

Business, predictably, is fighting these proposals and may succeed in delaying their enactment. But for once industry is wrong in opposing a union demand. Over the next few years American business will need redundancy planning much more than labor and will have to design it, develop it, and adopt it in its own self-interest. For American business needs to make some fast structural changes if it is to remain competitive, capable of growth, and profitable during a time of massive population shifts.

Neither government nor business is prepared for the peculiar demographic changes of the next few years. There will be sharp drops in the number of young people available for traditional manufacturing jobs and in the total number of people available for traditional work. These declines will result in part from the "baby bust" that began in 1960–61: In a few years the number of young people reaching working age will fall by almost 30 percent.

Equally important will be a qualitative shift resulting from the "educational explosion." Of the people who will reach retirement age in the next few years, fewer than a quarter will have completed high school. The majority went to work after no more than six or, at most, eight years of formal schooling. But of the young people entering the labor force, half will have been educated beyond high school and will therefore be unwilling to take traditional manual jobs. Indeed, they will be effectively disqualified for such jobs.

To create and find productive jobs for knowledge workers will be the first employment priority for this country. These had better be productive private-sector jobs; otherwise the political pressure for expanding governmental jobs will be well-nigh irresistible.

These demographic changes will require rapid automation and mechanization of existing processes. Automation can make many American manufacturing industries competitive again, precisely because this country possesses such a large supply of the knowledge workers who are needed to make automated plants productive. RCA, for example, recently built a plant that does what "everybody" had known was "absolutely impossible": It turns out color TV sets at lower cost than Japan or South Korea.

An even more important consequence of demography will be production sharing. Labor-intensive stages of production that cannot be automated or mechanized—sewing shirts, tanning hides, or assembling parts—will be carried out in the developing countries with their enormous and growing surplus of low-skilled young people qualified only for manufacturing work. American knowledge workers will handle the more technology-intensive and skill-intensive stages of production—design, engineering, quality control, and marketing.

Even Chrysler might become viable again if it followed this route. Indeed, Chrysler was a leader as long as it was based on production sharing, as it largely was before World War II. Then Chrysler confined itself, in the main, to design, engineering, and marketing. It bought parts and assembled them rather than manufacturing them. For many U.S. companies, production sharing will increasingly be the only way to stay in manufacturing, no matter how protectionist we might become. Production sharing has already become official policy in Japan. It is the fastest-growing mode of industrial organization in the world today. And it is growing quickly in America despite all resistance by government, by labor unions, and, incidentally, by manufacturers themselves.

Unless there is a severe and prolonged depression, the American economy in years to come will be marked more by a shortage than by a surplus of manual workers. Although the front pages may be dominated by horrible tales of unemployment, the numbers of people displaced by moves toward automation and production sharing will be small indeed compared to the total number of jobs. Chrysler, the country's tenth-largest manufacturer, employs fewer than 100,000 hourly workers out of a total American labor force of 100 million, or one tenth of 1 percent.

And, contrary to public belief, most workers laid off as the result of a structural or technological change manage to find new jobs fairly quickly. Even in steel towns where the dominant mill has shut down for good, more than four fifths of the affected employees have usually found new jobs within eighteen months, at least when overall economic conditions have been reasonably good.

Yet these small groups of "redundant" workers tend to be concentrated in small "distressed" areas. They tend to be middle-aged; old industries do not attract or hold many young people. These small groups are thus highly visible. They have political power out of all proportion to their numbers. And they are afraid.

What is worse, their plight infects the entire labor force with fear. Economically, one can argue that redundancy is not a problem.

Politically, it is a sizable problem. And psychologically and emotionally it is a dominant problem. If the fear of redundancy cannot be allayed, there will be massive resistance.

Whatever form it takes, this resistance will be futile, as the British experience amply proves. Subsidizing redundant workers and obsolete processes has not saved British automobile plants, shipyards, and steel mills. On the contrary, it has accelerated their decline. But it has also inhibited the development of employment-creating new industries and of competitive technologies.

There are three approaches in the world today to redundancy. The oldest is unemployment insurance—sixty-five years old in Great Britain, the country of its origin. Economically it has been a vast success. But psychologically it has been a failure. It does not do what it was primarily designed to do: give emotional security.

Then there is Japanese lifetime employment. Though enjoyed by less than a quarter of the Japanese labor force, it has, in the past, given emotional security to the whole of Japanese society. But economically it threatens to turn into a disaster, as it greatly impedes the shift from old to new technologies and from old to new industries. Indeed, Japan is now desperately engaged in finding a solution that will maintain the emotional security of lifetime employment and yet permit, even encourage, rapid shifts of labor.

The third, and newest, approach is best exemplified by Belgium, where laying off people with any seniority costs so much as to be prohibitive. But the Belgian practice actually creates the unemployment it is meant to combat. If they weren't afraid of being unable to lay off unneeded employees in the future, Belgian businesses—according to some estimates—would increase their hirings by 20 percent. As it is, hardly anyone in Belgium, whether Belgian or foreigner, starts a new industry or opens a new office.

We will be saddled with the Belgian "solution" unless we develop redundancy planning that welcomes redundancies, indeed speeds them up. We need to anticipate layoffs: There is usually a two-year lead time between the identification of redundancy and the actual closing of a plant or a change in process. We need to find new employment opportunities for people likely to be laid off, retrain them, and then place them.

This sounds like a formidable problem. A national program would certainly be as massive a boondoggle as the assorted governmental retraining programs already are. But as a local program, redundancy planning is fairly easy and cheap. We know this because it has been done—twice.

The first time was in Japan, seventy-five years ago, when, after the Russo-Japanese War, the country faced massive structural change in its industrial structure. At that time, the Mitsui group—already the country's leading *"zaibatsu"* (that is "financial group"—the Japanese term for what we now call a "conglomerate") and largest private employer—committed itself not to lay off redundant employees but instead to place them in jobs with other and growing Mitsui companies.

The second time redundancy planning was done successfully was in Sweden between 1950 and 1970. The country then faced a tremendous change from a primarily preindustrial, raw-material-producing economy into a modern technological economy. Under the leadership of a trade union economist, Gösta Rehn, tripartite groups were set up in each region to encourage, anticipate, and speed up redundancy and then retrain and place the affected people. Sweden moved almost half its labor force into new positions in those twenty years without great difficulty and at a fraction of the cost of paying unemployment compensation.

As a rule only a minority of redundant workers need to be trained and placed. A large group, mostly younger people, may need some counseling and placement help; otherwise, they have the required mobility. Another, and even larger, group is ready for early retirement, which usually means that they will find part-time jobs to bring their incomes back to their old standard. Only the middle-aged with large family obligations, limited skills, and low mobility need the assurance that they will be trained and placed.

What is needed is emotional rather than economic security. And this, as the Japanese and Swedish experiences have shown, only management can provide. American management must take the lead in fostering the emotional security of redundancy planning. If it does not, the fears of some very small groups may prevent American businesses from making the structural and technological changes that our population shifts and our technological opportunities demand.

(1979)

CHAPTER THIRTY-ONE

The Job as Property Right

IN EVERY DEVELOPED NON-COMMUNIST country, jobs are rapidly turning into a kind of property. The mechanism differs from culture to culture; the results are very much the same.

In Japan there is lifetime employment for the permanent (that is, primarily, male) employee in government and large businesses. This means, in effect, that short of bankruptcy the business is run primarily for the employee, whose right to the job has precedence over outside creditors and legal owners alike.

In Europe, increasingly, employees cannot be laid off; they have to be bought out with redundancy payments. In a few countries, such as Belgium and Spain, these payments can be so large as to be equivalent to a full salary or wage over the remainder of an employee's lifetime for a worker with long years of seniority. And the High Court of the European Community, in a decision which is considered binding in all member countries, has ruled that the claim to redundancy payments survives even an employer's bankruptcy and extends to the other assets of the owners of the employing firm.

In the United States recent legislation has given the employee's pension claim a great deal of the protection traditionally reserved for property. Indeed, in the event of bankruptcy or liquidation of the employing firm, employee pension claims take precedence over all other claims (except government taxes) for up to 30 percent of the employing firm's net worth.

The various fair-employment regulations in the United States, whether on behalf of racial minorities, women, the handicapped, or the aged, treat promotion, training, job security, and access to jobs as a matter of rights. It's getting harder to dismiss any employee except "for cause." And there is growing pressure, including a bill before Congress, to make the employer responsible for finding the employee an equivalent job in the event of a layoff.

Jobs, in effect, are being treated as a species of property rather than as contractual claims.

Historically there have been three kinds of property: "real" property such as land; "personal" property such as money, tools, furnishings, and personal possessions; and "intangible" property such as copyrights and patents. It is not too farfetched to speak of the emergence of a fourth—the "property in the job"—closely analogous to property in the land in premodern times.

The property rights in the job, such as pension claims or lifetime employment, cannot be bought or sold, pawned or bequeathed. Nor can they be taken away from their "rightful owner." And this was pretty much the way the law treated property in land in medieval Europe and premodern Japan.

This parallel is no accident, I submit. The emergence of property rights in the job does not result from union pressures or government fiat; neither, for instance, had much to do with Japan's lifetime employment practices. Rather, what a Marxist would call the "objective forces of history" have dictated that first land and now jobs would be accorded the status of real property.

For the great majority of people in most developed countries, land was the true "means of production" until well into this century, often until World War II. It was property in land which gave access to economic effectiveness and with it to social standing and political power. It was therefore rightly called by the law "real" property.

In modern developed societies, by contrast, the overwhelming majority of the people in the labor force are employees of organizations—in the United States the figure is 93 percent—and the "means of production" is therefore the job. The job is not "wealth." It is not "personal property" in the legal sense. But it is a "right" in the means of production, an *ius in rem*, which is the old definition of real property. Today the job is the employee's means of access to social status, to personal opportunity, to achievement, and to power.

For the great majority in the developed countries today the job is also the one avenue of access to personal property. Pension claims are by far the most valuable assets of employees over fifty, more valuable, indeed, than all his other assets taken together—his share in his house, his savings, his automobile, and so on. And the pension claim is, of course, a direct outgrowth of the job, if not part of the job.

The evolution of the job into a species of property can be seen as a genuine opportunity. It might be the right, if not the only, answer to the problem of "alienation," which Marx identified a century and a quarter ago as resulting from the divorce of the "worker" from the "means of production."

But as the long history of land tenure abundantly proves, such a development also carries a real danger of rigidity and immobility. In Belgium, for instance, the system of redundancy payments may prevent employers from laying off people. But it also keeps them from hiring workers they need, and thus creates more unemployment than it prevents or assuages. Similarly, lifetime employment may be the greatest barrier to the needed shift in Japan from labor-intensive to knowledge-intensive industries.

How can modern economies cope with the emergence of job property rights and still maintain the flexibility and social mobility necessary for adapting quickly to changes? At the very least, employing organizations will have to recognize that jobs have some of the characteristics of property rights and cannot therefore be diminished or taken away without due process. Hiring, firing, promotion, and demotion must be subject to pre-established, objective, public criteria. And there has to be a review, a pre-established right to appeal to a higher judge in all actions affecting rights in and to the job.

Standards and review will, paradoxically, be forced on employers in the United States by the abandonment of fixed-age retirement. To be able to dismiss even the most senile and decrepit oldster, companies will have to develop impersonal standards of performance and systematic personnel procedures for employees of all ages.

The evolution of jobs into a kind of property also demands that there be no "expropriation without compensation," and that employers take responsibility to anticipate redundancies, retrain employees about to be laid off, and find and place them in new jobs. It requires redundancy planning rather than unemployment compensation.

In the emerging "employee society," employees through their pension funds, are beginning to own—and inevitably will also control—the large businesses in the economy. Jobs are becoming a nexus of rights and a species of property. This development is surely not what people mean when they argue about "capitalism," pro or con. But it is compatible with limited government, personal freedom, and the rational allocation of resources through the free market. It may thus be the effective alternative to the "state capitalism" of the totalitarians, which, under the name of "communism," makes government into absolute tyranny and suppresses both freedom and rationality.

(**1980**)

PART V

The Changing Globe

During the last thirty years the international economy has become a transnational world economy. Even the mightiest national economy is now only one competitor in the world economy and dependent for its economic well-being on its success in the world economy. Paradoxically, the only major developed country in the Free World which understands this is the most nationalist and protectionist one: Japan. That Japan, since the early 1950s, has steered her economic course by the constellations of the world economy rather than by domestic economic considerations, as Keynesian (or Friedmanite) economics demands, has been a major factor in Japan's exceptional economic performance.

As a result, the economic theories by which most developed nations guide their policies are rapidly becoming obsolete. "Demand-management" can only produce inflation when domestic, i.e., national fiscal and monetary policies, no longer truly control a national economy. Then, as the Japanese first saw twenty years ago, national policy must focus on investment. There can then be no national key currency anymore, and countries must move toward new forms of money that are transnational rather than extensions of national sovereignty. And the demographic changes under way which are forcing us to shift from traditional trade in goods to international integration by stages of production and production sharing will further put the world economy in the ascendant.

This is much too big a topic to be covered briefly. For more extensive treatment in some depth see my recent book, *Managing in Turbulent Times*. The articles selected for this volume do, however, strike major themes and introduce important new questions, ideas, and concepts.

CHAPTER THIRTY-TWO

The Rise of Production Sharing

THE NEWEST WORLD ECONOMIC TREND is production sharing. Although neither export nor import in the traditional sense, this is how it is still shown in our trade figures and treated in economic and political discussions. Yet it is actually economic integration by stages of the productive process.

Few people have heard of production sharing, but everyone who has a hand-held calculator is familiar with it. The semiconductors that do the calculating are "Made in America" and then shipped for assembly to a developing country such as South Korea or Singapore. The finished product is then marketed primarily in developed countries.

Traditional statistics show the calculators as "imports," but actually they are the way in which American-made electronics go to market, earn foreign exchange, and create American jobs. Indeed, the old eighteenth-century German term *Veredelungsverkehr* (upgrading trade) describes the transaction better than any of the familiar terms of international economics and international trade theory.

A similar example of integration by stages of production is the large European textile group that does spinning, weaving, and dyeing in the European Common Market—all automated, capital-intensive, and high-technology processes. Then it airlifts the cloth to Morocco, Malaya, or Indonesia where it is converted into garments, bedding, rugs, towels, upholstery fabrics, or curtains. Finally, it is airfreighted back and sold in European markets.

There is also the production sharing actively promoted by the government of Japan, under which a Japanese company exports an entire industrial plant and receives much of its payment in that plant's products, which are sold in Japan.

The developed countries are strong in management, capital and technology, and consumer purchasing power. The developing countries offer enormous and rapidly growing labor surpluses.

We lack figures on the size of this process. But major multinational banks estimate that the volume at least doubled between 1974 and 1977. [*1981 note:* And it has doubled again since, that is, between 1977 and 1981.] Some banks consider it so significant already as to justify setting up special units within their traditional international or corporate banking divisions to finance production sharing.

Production sharing is bound to grow, for behind it is an inexorable economic force: population dynamics. One can argue about employment and unemployment figures in the developed countries, which are indeed very confusing. Nevertheless, more than half of all the young people entering the labor force in developed countries have attended some school beyond high school, thus they are not available for traditional low- or semiskilled work.

In the developing countries, however, population dynamics are vastly different. There the babies who did not die in the late fifties and sixties when infant mortality dropped precipitously—by 60 percent or 70 percent in some areas—are now entering the labor force and need jobs. Mexico, for instance, will have to find almost three times the number of jobs for young new workers in each year between now and 2000 than the country ever created in any previous year.

Few of these young people are highly trained or highly skilled, but they are far better prepared than their parents were—and increasingly they are in the cities. Farming cannot possibly provide the necessary jobs. Land reform, whatever its emotional appeal, would in most places exacerbate the problem.

Only in very few countries, countries like Brazil that are well past the "development takeoff," is there much potential for rapid growth of the domestic market. Moreover, developing countries usually lack the population base, purchasing power, and capital necessary for rapid domestic growth. The only employment conceivable for the masses of new workers is producing for the consumer markets of the developed countries, which no longer have adequate unskilled labor.

Production costs in developing countries tend to be high, often a good deal higher than in the developed countries, despite relatively low cash wages. Productivity tends to be low, and managerial and governmental overhead costs are often astronomical. Moreover, production sharing has fairly high costs of its own—heavy management requirements, high cost of capital, and added transportation expenses.

What propels the move toward production sharing is thus not primarily lower costs but the shortage of people available for the traditional production work in the developed world. Almost all developed countries have structured unemployment compensation, seniority rules, and retirement plans so as to discourage manual workers from looking for jobs outside the industry that originally employed them.

Production sharing may, in the last quarter of this century, become as dominant in the world economy as the traditional multinational corporation became in the world economy of the last twenty years. Yet, paradoxically, the multinational that organizes production sharing will be more controversial than ever.

This is because production sharing offers developing countries their only real opportunity to provide the jobs and skills their people need. But this won't necessarily make them grateful, so that they are more likely to continue the old rhetoric the more dependent they become on the "wicked imperialists."

Still, many developing countries are rapidly adjusting their policies and their behavior. "Multinational" is still a dirty word in the developing countries, but their governments increasingly court the multinationals to build and run export industries—the products of which the multinational is then expected to market in the developed world.

Only fifteen years ago, in the early sixties, the countries on the west coast of South America, from Venezuela to Chile, solemnly joined the Andean Pact, designed to drive out the multinationals. Within the last few years, each of those countries has either repealed most of the Andean Pact laws or quietly discarded them.

In developed countries, production sharing threatens the very base of traditional unionism, which lies in the old manual manufacturing industries. It is indeed likely to create more jobs than it displaces, above all, jobs for better-educated workers who make up the new labor force. But displaced workers will be far more visible and will be concentrated in areas that are already declining. They will also tend to be older people with limited skills. The same will largely be true of the businesses that employ these workers: yesterday's businesses in already declining industries.

Multinationalism will thus once more become a major issue in the developed countries. Indeed, the main attack against the multinational has already shifted from host countries to home countries, especially to the United States. Congress, the Internal Revenue Service, the Securities & Exchange Commission, and a host of other government agencies now pose even greater threats to multinationals than did either de Gaulle or Third World nationalism.

Therefore, we badly need policies enabling the economy to adopt production sharing at minimum cost to displaced workers.

We need the kind of policy the Swedes pioneered to make possible a similar transition from an almost preindustrial, raw-material-producing nation of the 1940s into the highly industrialized and highly competitive nation of today. Twenty years ago they organized employers, unions, and governments to work together to retrain redundant workers and place them in new jobs (an approach that accomplishes much more than any unemployment compensation system at a fraction of the cost).

We also need to revise the trade figures so that they enable us to know where production sharing creates and where it displaces jobs. Free trade or protectionist arguments only add to the confusion, for both assume an exchange of goods rather than economic integration by stages of production in which exports and imports are mutually dependent.

But the new, emerging multinational integration poses equally great challenges to management.

It does not fit the traditional organization structure of the multinational corporation, with a central top management to which management of subsidiaries reports. It requires, rather, a systems approach, in which one body coordinates autonomous managements that do not report to one another.

The new multinational does not rest on capital investment or ownership. In fact, the parent company in the developed country typically invests little or nothing, although it often provides its partners in the developing country access to financial resources by purchasing their output. For this reason, those that are likely to do best as new multinationals may well be marketing businesses rather than, as in the past, manufacturing businesses.

Smaller businesses are also likely to do better than giant companies, since they have the necessary flexibility. This explains why some medium-sized businesses are doing well in electronics.

A major requirement is the ability and willingness to adapt to different cultures and to work with people of different habits and traditions. For production sharing is not only transnational, rather than multinational; it is, above all, transcultural. And it is an idea whose time has come.

(1977)

CHAPTER THIRTY-THREE

Japan's Economic Policy Turn

JAPAN IS FACING THE MOST SERIOUS challenges to its traditional social and employment practices since World War II, if not since the 1920s. The reasons are neither politics nor economics but demographics.

The nation is only slowly climbing out of its worst recession in more than thirty years and the worst is yet ahead for the already bleak unemployment picture. And yet the Japanese business leaders, bankers, government and labor leaders with whom I met on my most recent visit to their country were fully as concerned with tomorrow's looming labor *shortage* as with today's traumatic unemployment.

Japan faces an almost total drying up of the labor supply on which the economic expansion of the twenty-five years after 1950 had been based: manufacturing workers. The problem may radically affect Japan's position in international trade and its export and import policies. It will challenge the nation's fundamental social beliefs and practices and will call for a rethinking of basic economic policy.

The number of young people reaching working age in Japan each year during the next twenty years will be 40 to 45 percent lower than it was during the sixties. Then half of the country's young people went to work after finishing junior high school.

Today practically everyone goes to high school and a full third of the high school graduates of both sexes (one half of the men) go on to college, against one eighth twenty-five years ago.

The Japanese rarely do things by halves and the swings there are much greater than in the United States. The Japanese postwar "baby boom" not only was sharper than in the United States but it was over much sooner, in the early 1950s. And then it was followed by a far more pronounced "baby bust"—a drop in the birthrate of over 40 percent, compared with a U.S. figure of 25 percent. Moreover, the economic and social consequences of these demographic trends are quite different in Japan and far greater.

One reason is the Japanese custom, almost amounting to sacred tradition, of tying wages and benefits to seniority. Over the course of thirty years of employment, the Japanese, whether working as machine tender, bookkeeper, or executive, triples his cash wage income. Fringe benefits such as housing allowances go up even faster. The employee with thirty years of seniority therefore costs the Japanese employer roughly four times as much as the newly hired young man or woman. The young people, in other words, subsidize the older people.

They also heavily subsidize the Japanese economy. Without any increase in wage rates, the labor costs of a Japanese organization, whether business, university, or government agency, go up automatically and sharply as employees get older. The more young people a company can hire, therefore, the lower will its labor costs be—and the more credit-worthy it will become in the eyes of Japanese banks. During the fifties and sixties the supply of young people was plentiful—partly from "baby boom" effects and partly because young people left the farms and streamed into the cities. At the end of World War II more than half of Japan's population was still on the farm; that figure is now down to 10 percent or 12 percent, and it is primarily young people, of course, who have left.

With Japan's traditional structure of labor costs, this meant steady improvement in competitive position for Japanese business and the Japanese economy. Indeed, something like half of the much-vaunted increases in the productivity of Japanese industry probably was not really "productivity increase." It was simply the labor force getting younger for twenty years.

But from now on, the labor force will, of necessity, get older. Labor costs will therefore rise sharply and labor productivity will fall or at least sharply slow its increase.

The second reason why the demographic shift is more of a problem to Japan than to any Western country is the tradition which rigidly ties job level and opportunity to education. Only junior high school graduates are supposed to go into manual jobs, and especially into manufacturing jobs. High school graduates become clerks and office workers. University graduates become managers and professionals. There has always been some, though not very much, upward mobility in this otherwise rigid classification of the human race by school certificate.

Downgrading, that is taking a job beneath one's final degree, is, however, almost unthinkable. There are plenty of high school graduates eligible for office and sales jobs. There is a surplus of people with college degrees and eligible for managerial and professional jobs. But the three kinds of employment—manual work, clerical work, managerial work—are separate labor pools which do not communicate with each other no matter what the demand and supply. And junior high school graduates, i.e., young people eligible for manual work, have all but disappeared.

Finally, the Japanese system makes it very difficult to utilize existing labor surplus in one industry or trade for job opportunities in other areas. There is, in absolute terms, no labor shortage in Japan— even of people eligible by educational status for manual work. In fact, by American standards, Japan would be considered a country with substantial labor surpluses. For there is still a substantial preindustrial sector in Japanese manufacturing, a sector of small workshops producing the traditional goods of "old Japan"—pottery or bedding, for instance. And there, labor as a rule is quite inefficiently used, though today it is anything but cheap. There are also large labor surpluses of industrial workers in old industries, such as the textile or the clothing industry.

But these pools of surplus labor do not help much. They cannot be tapped because of the seniority-wage system in which wage corresponds to length of service. A thirty-year-old industrial worker who is being hired for the first time by an employer would have to be paid a starting wage—that is the wage of a sixteen- or seventeen-year-old—and yet he is thirty. He can neither, in effect, be paid the wage befitting his age nor the wage befitting his seniority—and this makes him almost unemployable. At the very least, it creates tremendous obstacles against job change and job mobility. This also explains why unemployment is such a terrible threat to the Japanese—a laid-off man can find work only as a temporary employee at a very much lower income and with little chance ever to become a permanent employee again.

One should never underrate the Japanese ability for social innovation. Throughout their history the Japanese have been exceptionally gifted at finding solutions to new social problems while still maintaining traditional Japanese values. And they are at it again. I ran, for instance, into a very simple and yet highly ingenious solution to the conundrum of how to pay a man who moves to a new employer after ten or twelve years of service with an old one. He does not quit his old company; he joins the new one on permanent loan from the old employer. This makes it possible to pay him the wage befitting his age without violating the principle that wage be paid according to length of service. Still, the demographic and educational shifts under way will challenge social beliefs and customs that most Japanese consider sacred.

The economic impacts of the demographic shift will be at least as great as the social ones. Labor costs will go up fast, even if rates rise only slowly or not at all. The escalation of labor costs with length of services—wages as well as benefits—is far too deeply entrenched in Japanese society to be eliminated or even greatly modified. Worse still, manual labor for new industries or for expansion of old ones will not be available at all. For a hundred years the Japanese economy has been based upon the exchange of the products of Japanese hands for foodstuffs and raw materials from the outside world. The demographic shifts will not affect Japan's dependence on food, petroleum, iron ore, or wood pulp. But they will make it increasingly difficult for Japan to pay for them through the exports of the manufactured goods with which Japan has been paying for its imports. And so Japan is beginning to reassess its economic policies at home and especially in the world market.

One response is a new emphasis on automation. In the United States the talk of the automated factory, so common fifteen or twenty years ago, largely died down in the seventies. In Japan, work on the automated factory is going on at full speed and in dead earnest. Government and industry, with the unions acquiescing, are jointly developing the first totally automated large manufacturing plant—a highly flexible and diversified machine-tool plant. It will not have a single worker on the production floor. Most of the processes needed for this plant have been designed and tested and are in the pilot stage. The entire plant is expected to be in full commercial production by 1983.

Several large manufacturers—in fields ranging from chemicals to shoes—told me that their objective was to be able to produce, ten years hence, either double their present output with the same number of manufacturing workers or 30 to 40 percent more with half the present manual labor force. This, of course, will mean greatly increased employment of university-trained people, especially of engineers. But these the Japanese educational system provides in increasing quantities.

Another response is a deliberate shift, again with government and business working together to change the export mix. Increasingly, Japan expects to shift from exporting commodities, even those with high-technology content, to exporting entire plants and industries. The first export priority MITI, the powerful Ministry of

International Trade and Industry, announced recently will be the exportation of entire factories. In 1975 exports of factories amounted to $6 billion. The target for 1976 is double that. And by 1980 some Japanese planners hope to meet a $50 billion export target for complete factories [*1981 note:* which they almost hit]. With this, however, will also go a shift in the direction of Japanese trade. For the market for complete factories is, of course, not primarily the developed countries but the developing ones: the oil-rich countries, especially Saudi Arabia; the raw material and food-producing countries of Latin America; and perhaps most important, mainland China with its promise of a rapidly expanding petroleum production [*1981 note:* which did not materialize].

And finally, what Japan *imports* is likely to change—though politically this will be the most difficult of all the changes ahead. To export enough to provide a raw-material-poor, food-deficient, and energy-poor Japan with the foundations of modern economic life must remain the first priority of Japanese business policy. But increasingly Japan will have to export to pay for consumer goods from labor-surplus countries, consumer goods which its own labor-short economy can no longer produce. The shoe factory which a Japanese company is now building, for instance, in one of the countries of Southeast Asia will be paid for out of its own output—with 10 percent or 20 percent of its production turned over at cost for twenty years to the Japanese who financed and built the factory. This, on the one hand, makes possible building a plant that has economies of scale beyond the absorptive capacity of the small country in which it will be located. It creates, on the other hand, a source of consumer goods based on abundant labor supply and fairly low labor costs for the Japanese home market and for the Japanese consumer.

Whether such a policy shift can actually work is by no means certain yet. In Japan it will be opposed bitterly by the labor unions, but also by the exceedingly numerous and powerful small businesses. It requires a complete about-face on the part of the Japanese

Government, and especially of the Ministry of International Trade and Industry. For it is still axiomatic at MITI that anything that Japan is technically capable of producing must be produced in Japan and must not be brought in from the outside. And MITI reflects deeply held national convictions that go back almost four hundred years.

Outside of Japan there are also formidable obstacles. While Japan would offer developing countries a chance to speed up their own industrialization, it would make them heavily dependent on Japan; a small Southeast Asian country would, in effect, become a Japanese satellite. But, as a highly placed Japanese observed to me, "What alternative do we have, considering our population trend? And what alternative do the developing countries—especially small, poor, and overpopulated ones—have, considering their population dynamics?"

Whichever way Japanese economic policy finally goes, demographics—both in respect to the number of people and to their education—will increasingly become a key factor, if not the controlling factor, in the Japanese economy and in Japan's position in, and policy toward, the world economy.

(1976)

CHAPTER THIRTY-FOUR

The Battle Over Co-Determination

ONE OF THE MOST IMPORTANT social and political disputes in Western Europe these past few years is the battle over co-determination.

Basically, co-determination is the legal system that grants trade unions substantial or controlling membership on boards of directors or on company supervisory boards. In various ways it is the law for larger companies in Germany, Holland, and Scandinavia, and it is under active discussion in Great Britain, Belgium, and France.

In discussing with me the political battle over co-determination, a senior official in the German Ministry of Labor recently said that in his country the new managerial and professional groups are rapidly becoming the majority in postindustrial society. As a result, the unions are trying desperately to deny those groups power and to disenfranchise them before the unions lose too much membership to the middle class.

This, he explained, is why the unions, in their push for employee representation on boards of directors, so adamantly refuse to accept any representatives of middle management and insist on confining board membership to union officers who represent blue-collar workers.

A German trade union official whom I saw during the same trip did not deny this. "Even if they unionize," he said, "managerial and professional people are not really 'workers.' If we allow them a say on company boards, they will always vote with management; and if we do not establish a principle that only bona fide workers have the right to share in the control of business, the labor movement will soon become yesterday."

At the same time (i.e., in spring, 1977), across the English Channel, everybody was talking about the Bullock Report, the work of a ten-man British Royal Commission headed by Oxford historian Lord (Allan) Bullock, the biographer of Adolf Hitler and Ernest Bevin.

The Bullock Report caused widespread reverberations when it was released in January of 1977. It recommended that the boards of British companies that employ two thousand or more people, including British units of multinational companies based outside the United Kingdom, be refashioned to give workers the same number of representatives as stockholders, providing one third of the company's employees wanted such representation.

The committee majority said that labor representation in the boardroom (so-called industrial democracy) was already the wave of the present. Moreover, it said such representation would provide a new legitimacy for the exercise of the management function within an agreed policy framework.

The head of Britain's major labor confederation agreed, predicting the Bullock Report would become "a landmark in the development of our democratic institution." But the nation's principal employer group denounced the report, saying that if enacted it would fundamentally change Britain's free enterprise system.

Both the German trade unionist and the Bullock Report went too far. The Germans were forced to accept middle-management people on the supervisory board and indeed had to agree to grant them a controlling vote in the legislation that went into effect in Germany in 1977.

And the uproar caused by Bullock's admitted discrimination against managerial and professional people explains why that report's proposals have been shelved in Great Britain.

But it would be foolish to believe that labor in either country has given up the attempt to disenfranchise management and professional people. In fact, German labor's first priority is to repeal the provisions of the co-determination law that mandate representation of management people on boards of supervisors. Avowed Socialists, after all, need to believe in the concept of economic-class warfare and find it difficult to cope with the fact of an emerging managerial and professional class.

European trade unionists and their Socialist allies want to disenfranchise managers to prevent their becoming powerful in business and society. Yet this may be their undoing. A good many people in the Socialist parties of Germany, Scandinavia, the Low Countries, and in Great Britain with whom I talked during a European trip in the spring of 1977 felt that the German co-determination battle and the British uproar over the Bullock Report might eventually end middle-class support for Labor or Socialist parties.

"The young management people in this country," said a middle-of-the-road labor minister in Britain, "still do not like the Tories. But, after Bullock, they probably like Labor even less—and they may have shifted away from us for good, and not only for the next election."

Thus it seems apparent that co-determination, even where it is merely debated and then set aside, is an explosive issue that has important political as well as social and economic ramifications. We in this country would do well to pay greater attention to this issue. [*1981 note:* And indeed, three years after this article was first published, the United Automobile Workers began to demand co-determination as its price for supporting an ailing Chrysler.]

(**1977**)

CHAPTER THIRTY-FIVE

A Troubled Japanese Juggernaut

SEEN FROM THE UNITED STATES, Japan has a record—and mounting—surplus in her balance of payments and in her international trade. Seen from Japan, this "surplus" looks more like a record write-off of massive inventory losses.

Seen from the United States, the Japanese yen is the strongest among free world currencies, perhaps still undervalued at 250 to the dollar and kept from rising further only by the "dirty float"—large-scale intervention by the Bank of Japan. Seen from Japan, the strength of the yen looks transitory and illusionary.

Seen from the United States, Japanese economic policy looks only too successful—a commercial juggernaut that knows no bounds. Seen from Tokyo, Japan is now beginning to face up to the consequences of monumental economic and business blunders that threaten to sink, or at least slow, the juggernaut.

The Japanese businessmen and government officials who attended a round of seminars and meetings that I conducted in Japan in the summer of 1977—the tenth such visit in eighteen years—are all singing the blues. On the surface there would seem little evidence for their concern. Restaurants and bars are crowded;

not a room was to be had in any resort, and planes and trains were sold out on National Culture Day, November 3; consumer buying is at an all-time peak; merchants expect a record Christmas selling season.

As to unemployment, the official figure is less than 2 percent.

Yet Japanese businessmen and government officials may have ample grounds for their malaise, though not for the reasons they often give in public.

In the first place, Japan is grossly overstocked with high-priced inventories of industrial materials. "We usually keep five to six months of inventory of glass-making sand," the president of one of the big glass companies told me. "Now we have enough for three years of full production." The husband of a friend of ours, a middle-level executive in a textile firm, goes to work every morning and sits at his desk for ten hours doing little but reading detective stories; he is a production manager and the firm hasn't produced anything in five months because all its warehouses are bulging with unsold merchandise.

In October 1977, Japan and Australia settled their "sugar war." The Japanese sugar refineries had contracted in 1974 to buy the entire Australian sugar crop for 1976 and 1977 at the high prices then prevailing—five to eight times current prices. When the Australians started to deliver, the Japanese balked on their commitments. At one point 150 ships were tied up in Tokyo Harbor waiting to unload sugar.

The Japanese finally caved in after the Australians made a token concession to extend the payments period from three to four years. Now the Japanese are stuck with two years of supply at the highest prices ever recorded for sugar.

The same is true of copper, iron ore, pulp, sulphur, and coking coal. The Japanese, and above all Japanese officialdom, were seized by hysteria in 1974 when raw materials shortages were cropping up everywhere. They bought and bought and bought. Now they are frantically trying to get out of commitments to take delivery and have slashed raw materials imports nearly in half. Even so, industrial inventories are bulging with high-priced raw materials. (Apparently the same thing is happening with some finished goods: Another friend recounts that his government ministry still has a two-year supply of toilet paper as a result of the shortage scare several years ago.)

The second blunder by the Japanese was committed in 1975 and 1976. Japanese industry not only kept on producing when world demand went down, it actually stepped up production in many cases. The need to maintain employment was responsible only in part, and probably in lesser part.

The main reason was miscalculation. The Japanese, and, again, government officials in particular, expected a speeding up of world inflation and a very rapid recovery of demand in Japan's markets, especially in Europe. "We made a deliberate decision to step up production," says the executive vice president of a battery company. "We expected world prices to go up 30 percent. They have gone down instead, and by the middle of 1976 we had the equivalent of two full years of sales in our warehouses."

When the banks began to put on the screws for repayment of inventory loans, Japan's export drive went into high gear. But the inventories of finished goods for many industries—steel, textiles, consumer electronics—are still very high.

The final blunder was the Japanese response to their predicament. Partly by consensus among government, business, and labor unions, which are far more closely knit in Japan than in other industrialized nations, and partly because of the politics of the situation, the Japanese decided to keep domestic prices high and push exports. Exports are being priced to sell rapidly; higher returns from domestic sales are being used to compensate for export losses.

There have been exceptions. Akio Morita, for instance, the head of Sony Corporation, is known to have been highly critical of such a policy. Sony, perhaps alone among major Japanese companies, has lowered its prices in Japan while raising them in the export market.

Japanese business leaders realized that their strategy risked provoking extreme protectionist reaction from abroad. But politically the strategy was irresistible, particularly to the labor unions. It seemed to be the only way to enable business to keep on raising wages and benefits. In 1975, for example, wages and benefits went up almost 40 percent, enabling consumers to pay some of the highest prices in the world. (Low-grade beef sells for $15 to $20 a pound in Tokyo, fish is almost as expensive, and *matsutake*, the popular Japanese mushrooms, are going for as high as $40 a pound.)

Now, however, Japan faces a protectionist backlash of major proportions, as is rapidly becoming clear in the United States. And her own protectionist policies have pushed up the yen to where Japan is rapidly becoming one of the highest-cost producers among industrial countries. A good deal of excess inventory still hasn't been worked down, and yet Japan faces the prospect of being forced to curtail exports sharply or lose permanent access to major world markets.

Easing agricultural protection—perhaps by switching from a system of restricting imports to a system of subsidizing farm incomes directly, as in the United States or Britain—would go some way toward shrinking Japan's balance-of-trade surplus. It would also reduce the threat to Japan's ability to compete posed by exorbitant food costs and consequent wage demands. So far, however, there have been only token concessions—to New Zealand, for example, which threatened to forbid Japanese fishermen access to her fishing grounds unless given better access to the Japanese market for meat and dairy products.

More heroic measures are needed. One may be to conduct a genuine clearance sale by selling a very large amount of inventory at low prices and on favorable credit terms to nonmarket countries, especially Red China.

This is the way in which the battery manufacturer mentioned above cleared his inventory. The trouble is that there isn't too much that Japan makes that China needs in quantity; the Chinese demand for color TVs, for example, is likely to be limited, to say the least. Still, Japanese steel, chemicals, and plastics might find a market in China and perhaps also the Soviet Union. A major trade deal in the near future with those countries wouldn't be a surprise.

But, above all, expect a period of turbulence in Japanese economic and currency policy. The adjustments that the Japanese have to make are fairly obvious—but they also are going to be very painful, financially as well as politically.

(1977)

CHAPTER THIRTY-SIX

India and Appropriate Technology

"THE BIG MISTAKE GANDHI made was to advocate the spinning wheel," said one influential Indian government economist. "It's much too efficient. With the unemployment and underemployment we have in our villages the truly appropriate technology is the hand-held spindle, the spinning whorl." Yet this is hardly how the Indian villagers define "appropriate technology" for themselves.

What struck me most when traveling in the winter of 1978–79 for six weeks through rural India was not the pervasive poverty or the palpable unemployment; I had expected both. What I had not expected, however, were the four or five brand-new bicycles standing outside every one of the miserable hovels—and not one of them chained or locked. There may still be more bullock carts in rural India than bicycles; there surely are still infinitely more bullock carts than there are small tractors. But what powers India's Green Revolution, what has given the subcontinent a food surplus for the first time in its thousands of years, is not the digging stick or the wooden plow. It is the ubiquitous gasoline pump in the tub well and the irrigation ditch of an arid land.

From every bullock cart, every camel cart, every pedicab, and every howdah on the back of an elephant there issue the strains of the transistor radio. And the most crowded stand in every one of the countless village markets is the one that sells motor scooters on the installment plan.

Much as it pains the Indian government economist and his boss, the Prime Minister, the bicycle, transistor radio, gasoline pump, and motor scooter—rather than the spinning wheel, let alone the distaff or the spinning whorl—are indeed the appropriate technology for India and for most developing countries. They create jobs and purchasing power—the distaff would destroy both.

No one in India could tell me what the economic policy of the government is. The only governmental actions are expansion of already large government enterprises, unchecked growth of an already obese bureaucracy, and more bureaucratic regulations. The cabinet cannot agree on anything and has no policy whatever. Substantial sums are being allocated to the villages but without programs, let alone goals. But there is a pervasive rhetoric of smallness and of antitechnology.

India's Prime Minister at the time of my trip (i.e., before Mrs. Gandhi's return to power), Morarji Desai, eighty-four years old but looking fifty-five (which he attributes to his eating only raw mashed vegetables and drinking his own urine), preached to me "small is beautiful," "rural development," and "appropriate [that is, preindustrial] technology." It is this rhetoric that his economic adviser echoes when he counsels a return to the spinning whorl. And pretty much the same rhetoric can now be heard in many developing countries, for example in Indonesia or from the Islamic fundamentalists in Iran. It is very much the same rhetoric that underlay the disastrous Great Leap Forward in Maoist China twenty years ago, with its emphasis on the village and on backyard steel furnaces.

As a reaction to the delusion of "the bigger the better," which enthralled earlier Indian governments, especially Nehru, Desai's emphasis on rural India was overdue. Earlier governments neglected the village, where 90 percent of India's 550 million people still live. But "small is beautiful" is just as much a delusion as "the bigger the better." What is appropriate is not what uses the most capital or the most labor; it is not what is "small" or "big," "preindustrial" or a "scientific marvel." What is appropriate is quite simply what makes the economy's resources most productive. What is appropriate in a country of huge population and rapid population growth is what multiplies productive jobs. What is development in a country which like India has sizable resources of managerial and entrepreneurial skill and at the same time huge unfulfilled consumer needs is whatever creates purchasing power.

Steel mills, those prestige investments of the 1960s into which earlier Indian governments poured very large chunks of the country's scarce capital resources, are becoming the white elephants of the 1970s and 1980s. Steel mills are inappropriate technology for a country like India. They are highly capital-intensive rather than labor-intensive. They supply a commodity which is in ample supply on the world market and available everywhere at a low price. Above all, they create practically no jobs beyond those in the mill itself.

But the automotive industry—passenger cars, motorbikes, trucks, and tractors—is probably the most efficient multiplier of jobs around. Its own plants have a fairly high ratio of labor to capital, and the industry generates about four to five secondary or tertiary jobs throughout the economy for every one in the manufacturing plant. It creates jobs in road building and road maintenance, in traffic control, in dealerships, service stations, and repair work. And it creates enormous purchasing power with these jobs.

Similarly, making transistor radios and bicycles requires both a large manufacturing base and a large dealer system; and both multiply jobs and create purchasing power. And like the automotive industry, both create human capital, that is, skills accessible to the unlearned. The same might be said for the manufacture of synthetic fertilizer or pharmaceuticals or pesticides—all require big enterprises and national distribution and service (moreover, these products, together with the gasoline pump, underlie the two great successes of India since independence: the rapid increase in food production and the rapid decrease in infant mortality).

Equally appropriate as a creator of productivity, jobs, and purchasing power is the cosmetics manufacturer, who may be quite small. I saw a highly efficient and highly successful multinational cosmetics firm in Bangalore which, with twenty employees, produces five times as much foreign exchange per rupee of investment or sales as any of the huge state-owned Indian enterprises.

The development decades of the fifties and sixties worshiped capital investment. The best testament to this superstition is *The Stages of Economic Growth*, which Walt W. Rostow, later President Johnson's foreign policy adviser, wrote in the early 1960s and which then became the bible of the developing countries. Mr. Rostow proclaimed that development is an automatic and direct function of the size of capital investment. But that is not productivity; it's waste and incompetence. Today there is a tendency to define productivity as whatever uses the most labor—especially in the developing countries, with their huge, unemployed, young population.

But that, too, is incompetence. Productivity is whatever generates the highest overall yield from an economy's resources of capital, labor, physical resources, and time. This will also give the largest number of jobs and the maximum purchasing power. It will even produce the lowest possible inequality in the distribution of incomes attainable at a given stage of economic development. And surely poor countries cannot afford to support unproductive people—that is, people who appear busy winding a few strands of cotton around a wooden staff. Rich countries may be able to keep unproductive people gainfully unemployed, but poor countries have no surplus to distribute.

Above all, the troubadours of "small is beautiful" forget—as does so much of official Washington—that a healthy economy and society need *both* the large and the small. Indeed, the two are interdependent in both a developed and developing country. There can be no small manufacturer in a large market—whether that of the United States or of India—unless there is a large assembler or a large retailer, an IBM, a GM, a Sears Roebuck. It is only in their products or their stores that the small man's output can reach the market. But there would also be no GM except for the existence of a multitude of small autonomous tool-and-die shops and a host of small parts suppliers, or local dealers, service stations, and repair shops.

Pharmaceutical research requires big—if not very big—enterprises. But pharmaceutical sales depend on some 200,000 drugstores and 200,000 physicians—each of necessity decentralized and indeed autonomous. Rural development in India not only means national marketing organizations for village products and national credit and banking institutions. It means huge power stations. Above all—something the advocates of "small is beautiful" always conveniently overlook—it means centralized government bureaucracies, which surely could not be called "small" whether or not they deserve to be called "beautiful."

None of these arguments, I am afraid, made much impact on the Indian government economist—nor, I realized, would they have made much impact on his Prime Minister. But once Indians have the bicycle, the motor scooter, the transistor radio, and the gasoline pumps, are they really going to go back to the spinning whorl?

(1979)

CHAPTER THIRTY-SEVEN

Toward a New Form of
Money?

SINCE 1973, WHEN FLOATING exchange rates first became the new orthodoxy, two schools of economic thought have been arguing with each other.

One, the majority, believes floating exchange rates are necessary and permanently desirable. This school would consider any return to fixed rates potentially catastrophic because of the periodic crises that seem to build up when governments are charged with adjusting the rates.

The other school, today in the minority, believes that floating exchange rates only encourage fiscal irresponsibility and inflation. It argues for a return to fixed rates as a means of forcing governments to keep their money supplies under control.

The two schools appear to be incompatible. Yet we may well be halfway toward a two-tier monetary and currency structure that institutionalizes both views. One tier would be national currencies issued and manipulated by national governments and floating in relation to each other. The other tier would be a transnational currency consisting of money of account held by the world banking system and denominated in terms of its purchasing power.

Most of the world's economy's business and trade is now carried on in "Eurocurrencies"—Eurodollars, Euromarks, Euroyen, Euroswissfrancs, and so on. The textbooks originally defined Eurodollars as dollars deposited in American banks but held abroad. But that definition long ago ceased to bear any relationship to reality. The Eurodollar—or the Euromark or the Euroyen or the Euroswissfranc—is purely transnational money, owned by anyone and deposited anywhere. Commonly, Eurocurrencies are created when a company or individual, perhaps to gain a higher interest rate, makes a deposit in another country.

The Eurodollar became popular in the mid-1960s when President Johnson first retreated from the key-currency role of the U.S. dollar by imposing restrictions on American investment abroad. But it was invented—and this is a delicious irony—by the Soviet state bank in the 1950s when the Soviets withdrew dollars on deposit in the United States, placed them in their London branch, and began making loans based on them. The Soviet intent was to insulate the deposits from being blocked by U.S. Government action; the result was a financial instrument that may have saved the world economy and indeed the free-market system.

It was assumed in the 1960s that Eurodollars would remain a minor adjunct to national and nationally regulated currencies. It was also assumed that the U.S. dollar would remain solid and that the U.S. Government would have both the will and the resources to maintain its internal and external value.

Both were rational assumptions fifteen years ago. Both have been disproven by events. The Eurocurrencies have become the dominant money of the world economy—with national currencies rapidly becoming the adjuncts. There were, in 1979, $900 billion of Eurocurrency in circulation in the world's banking system—$600 billion if interbank loans are deducted. [1981 note: The figure is substantially higher now.] This is more than all the national bank deposits of the world's developed free-market countries.

But it is surely also abundantly clear by now that every modern government must be expected to put domestic and short-range considerations—employment, the protection of dying industries, the competitive position of its exports—before concern from the outside world, even though it is of course the world economy that today lays the golden eggs for the developed countries. There cannot, in other words, any longer be any one "key currency" which can be confidently expected to be stable or even predictable for any length of time.

To be sure, some of the authors of the new European currency union, the European Monetary System, which is just making its first tentative and halting steps, are hoping that a European currency based on the German mark will become the monetary and trading support of the world economy. But as the very able German Minister of Finance, Hans Matthofer, said in Frankfurt in the summer of 1979, this assumes (a) that the United States will keep the dollar stable rather than subordinate its foreign exchange value to domestic considerations of employment and of the balance of trade; (b) that the French will be willing to defend the franc at the risk of substantial unemployment; and (c) that the British, under the Conservative government, will do likewise.

Mr. Matthofer thought these reasonable assumptions "for the short term"—but this is hardly good enough to base the future of the world economy on. [*1981 note:* And clearly Mr. Matthofer was wrong even "for the short term."]

There are two responses to the development of Eurocurrencies. The first is to attempt to undo it. This is, in effect, what the U.S. Government was aiming at during the Carter Administration, with its well-publicized proposals to force the "stateless money" of the Eurodollar market back under the jurisdiction and regulation of U.S. monetary and financial authorities. That attempt was doomed to fail. Only the Germans supported it, and none too ardently. The British, French, and Japanese governments had no use for it. And if the United States and the Germans had succeeded in emasculating the present system the lenders would, it is quite clear, have designed a new one, as their predecessors, fifteen years ago, had designed the Eurodollar.

The second response is coming from the main lenders in the Eurocurrency markets, the OPEC countries, and the multinationals based in countries with substantial trade surpluses, primarily West Germany and Japan. Those lenders are pushing hard for a shift to a truly transnational currency. They need money that is not tied to any one denomination but linked to purchasing power— e.g., through guaranteed convertibility at fixed rates into a "market basket" of other currencies, through indexing according to the wholesale or manufacturers' price index of leading industrial countries, or, perhaps, through something like the traditional gold clause of the nineteenth century.

On a 1979 trip through Europe's main economic centers almost every banker and government economist—in London, Frankfurt, Brussels, Madrid, and Stockholm—talked to me of the shift to such a transnational Eurocurrency as all but inevitable.

As one large banker noted, the OPEC countries have stuck with the dollar for political reasons. How much longer can they afford to do so, considering the rapid depreciation of the dollar and the equally rapid escalation in prices they pay to the industrial world for finished goods? In fact, before the Iranian crisis pushed oil prices way up in 1979 the purchasing power of what OPEC received for its oil had fallen to what it was before the OPEC cartel became effective in 1973. That OPEC's own actions are largely responsible for this, and that old and well-proven economic theory has long taught that a cartel cannot and will not increase the real income of its industry members unless there is a genuine physical shortage of the product and of the capacity to produce it, is not seen or admitted by the OPEC countries.

Thus even the most responsible and most intelligent members of OPEC see themselves as almost forced to demand that their money on deposit in the world banking system be kept in a form that protects it against expropriation through currency devaluation on the part of the developed world, that is, in a transnational currency. And a German banker in Frankfurt said almost the same thing when talking of his clients, the large German multinationals and their export business.

How fast will the shift come and how far will it go? "Within three years," said a banker with Arab connections, "one third of the new currency deposits will have become nonnational in their denomination through one device or another." The banker in Frankfurt thought this to be high—one fifth was more likely in his opinion. [*1981 note:* The Frankfurt banker was about right.]

Perhaps most plausible was the assessment of the London top executive of one of the big American banks. "The shift has just begun," he said, "but the trend is sharply upward. And thus the banks will have to put the same purchasing power safeguards on the loans they make against Eurodeposits. We are good at hedging against currency risks—we have to be good. But no one is good enough to hedge against even one tenth of his deposits. And so the loans the banks make will also be in a transnational currency rather than the banks taking on the risk of national currencies themselves." [*1981 note:* That began in 1980.]

In the early 1940s, John Maynard Keynes began to advocate a truly transnational money which he called "Bancor" and which he proposed to have managed by a transnational, nonpolitical group of bankers and economists. His proposal was defeated by the American Keynesians at the Bretton Woods Conference of 1944, in part because of their suspicion of "British Imperialism," in part because they wanted the dollar to become the world's key currency and were convinced that it could play that role, despite Keynes' warnings that a "key currency" had become a dangerous self-delusion. Then, in the mid-seventies that arch-non-Keynesian, F. A. Hayek, proposed that governments get out of money completely and turn the job over to individual and competing banks, with the market deciding which bank's money it was willing to trust.

Neither proposal is likely to become reality. We know today that Keynes greatly overrated the capacity of the "value-free expert" to make nonpolitical decisions and to impose them on national governments. And Hayek's proposal is unlikely to be accepted in the foreseeable future by politicians, parliaments, or ministries of finance. But the assumption underlying these two proposals—that money is far too important to be entrusted to politicians and governments—is now accepted, I would say, by almost everyone (except perhaps ministers of finance). It is even increasingly accepted by ordinary people who know no economics but who see the purchasing power of their earnings decline month after month.

Surely no one, perhaps not even the ministers of finance, any longer believes, as we so blithely did when I attended the Keynes Seminar in Cambridge in the early thirties, that governments have both the competence and the integrity to manage money responsibly and nonpolitically.

Transnational money for the world economy, that is, money denominated in any one national currency but tied, one way or another, to purchasing power, is thus a logical and perhaps inescapable development. It is unlikely to be as orderly as Keynes' proposed Bancor would have been, or as rational as Hayek's free-market, competitive, bank money. It is going to be messy, difficult, complicated, risky, and cause endless friction. And as the history of central banking abundantly demonstrates, there are very real dangers in banks trying to be banks of issue that manage currency and commercial banks concerned with liquidity and profits. Two-tier currencies may be a cure worse than the disease.

But transnational money might work. With all its imperfections, it may well become reality in a world which demands both national currencies that are politically controlled and managed for short-term political expediency and transnational currency stable enough to finance trade and investment in an increasingly interdependent world economy.

(1979)

CHAPTER THIRTY-EIGHT

How Westernized Are the Japanese?

"I DETEST THE NEPOTISM THAT pervades Japanese academic life," says the distinguished historian. "Young scholars should make their careers on their merits and not on their family ties. That's why I married my four daughters to the ablest and brightest of my doctoral students. This way I could do what Japanese tradition expects and place my sons-in-law into the best of professorships—and I could do it with a good conscience for I know they deserve it."

"We are completely Western in this outfit," says the successful independent movie producer in his modernistic Tokyo studio. "We even have a woman vice president in charge of finance and administration. But, Professor Drucker, could you act as her go-between and find a husband for her in the United States? She is thirty now and should be married soon."

"It would be wonderful if you'd find an American husband for me and arrange the marriage," chimes in the attractive woman VP. "No Japanese will marry a women's libber like myself, who is a professional and executive." "Does it have to be an arranged marriage?" I ask. "Definitely," answers the women's libber, "the other way is much too risky."

"Young Ohira will be the chief executive of this company in ten to fifteen years," I had been told repeatedly by the chairman of one of the leading high-technology firms. But when I inquire about Ohira on my latest Japanese trip, there is embarrassed silence. "We had to let him go," the chairman says. "He is an oldest son and his father, who owns a small wholesale business in Kobe, demanded that he take over the family company. We tried to talk the old man out of it, but he is stubborn and so we had to let Ohira go."

"Did he want to leave?" I ask. "Of course not, but he had no choice. He could never have been promoted if he had stayed. Executives, after all, have to set an example—and in Japan an oldest son is still expected to follow his father in his business."

The young woman who interpreted for me at a press conference asks whether she and her biochemist husband might come and get my advice. Their problem? Interpreters are very well paid and so the young woman makes more than her husband, who, under Japanese seniority rules, won't be a full professor for six more years. Then their positions will be reversed. He'll make about three times what he makes now; and she plans to take time out to have children. But in the meantime both his and her family disapprove and nag.

"Does it bother you that the wife has the larger income?" I ask. "Not in the least," they both answer. "Then why do you have to tell your families?" I say. They beam, tell me I've saved their marriage, and thank me profusely. "Did you really need me to tell you that?" I ask. "Of course not," they say, "but this is Japan; to do anything unconventional you have to have a *sensei* [master] tell you so—and we were pretty sure what you'd tell us when we came for your advice."

There is thus a good deal to support the "old Japan hands" in their contention that the Japanese are Westernized "from nine to five" only. It is certainly a much safer assumption in dealing with Japanese than the advice I heard a Swiss banker give to his successor as the bank's representative in Tokyo: "Treat them as if they were American MBAs with German-sized attaché cases," let alone the wondrous description by a group of European Common Market economists that is quoted up and down Japan with mixed amusement and indignation: "The Japanese are economic animals who live in rabbit hutches."

"For twenty years," says an experienced executive recruiter, "I have placed Japanese executives with Western companies. The firms that have been successful in attracting and holding truly able Japanese are the ones who know that they'll behave like Japanese no matter how impeccable their English or how much they prefer whiskey to sake."

Indeed the Japanese—except "from nine to five"—may well have become more "Japanese" and less "Western" these last few years.

Ten or fifteen years ago, for instance, performances of the Noh—the traditional and stylized dance-opera—played to empty houses, with the few spectators mainly elderly men who came in, one suspected, because the place was air-conditioned. When I went to a Noh performance in June of 1980 it was sold out, with every seat taken, mostly by professionals or young executives by their looks.

But things are rarely that simple—and never in Japan. Consider, for instance:

The twenty-year-old daughter of old friends—we have known her since she was a toddler—tells us that she is majoring in philosophy. "Last term I took a nifty seminar reading Plato," she says. "Do you have good translations of Plato into Japanese?" I ask. "We don't read translations," she answers, quite indignant. "We read Plato in Greek. And this term we are reading Kant and Schopenhauer, in German. And I am also taking a very interesting course in Whitehead, Russell, Wittgenstein, and Symbolic Logic, in English, of course."

"And what are you doing for fun?" I ask. "But *this* is the fun," she answers. "Of course I also have to prepare myself for a job and for earning a living, and so I am doing judo. I got the Black Belt eighteen months ago and am now studying for the instructor's exam. I am already adviser to the judo club at my university and hope the university will hire me as a judo teacher when I graduate next year. Don't smirk," she cries. "I am in dead earnest. Japanese girls are now studying medicine and accounting and even engineering. But these are all imports from the West. To be accepted as equals our women will have to make it in something purely Japanese—and what could be more Japanese than judo?"

Miyeko, whom we first knew as a college sophomore who interpreted for us on a hiking and camping trip, visits us with her six-year-old daughter and her husband, a middle-level executive in a big trading company. She confides that they both very much want to have another child but have decided against it.

"It might be a boy and, of course, that's what we'd hope for," Miyeko says. "And then the firm would not send us overseas or would demand that I stay in Japan with the children and send him alone. You know that a Japanese boy has to grow up in Japan ever to be accepted as a Japanese. And my husband is in line, just now, for New York or Los Angeles." "Why do you want so badly to go abroad?" I ask. "Are the career opportunities better?"

"On the contrary," answers her husband. "If I stay in the home office I have a good chance to be in top management in ten years; if I go overseas I'll be tagged as a foreign specialist and never make it. But that's a cheap price to pay for the freedom one has outside of Japan. I can't tell you how much Miyeko and I enjoyed the seven years I was posted to Dusseldorf when we could go together in the evening to concerts or to the theater and could go hiking and camping on weekends. Now Japanese convention demands that we live with Miyeko's parents and they expect us to look after them on weekends. And I never see my wife and daughter. I have to sit and drink in a Ginza bar every night till eleven during the week, either with my bosses or with my subordinates. You can't imagine how sick and tired Miyeko and I are of all this never-ending Japanese togetherness. And all my colleagues who have served overseas feel the same way."

There is a revival under way of the old and charming Japanese custom of having one really good and expensive piece of art serve as the sole decoration of the small and bare Japanese apartment. But what the young couples now buy when they start out in their own home is rarely Japanese art; they buy a Picasso etching or pre-Columbian pottery from Mexico or Peru, or a miniature from Moghul India, or a terra-cotta figurine supposedly found in an Etruscan tomb.

When, on a hot June Sunday, I made my way through a traffic jam of strollers on the beaches south of Tokyo, there were, it seemed, the same young families—father, mother, and two children—that had been there twenty years earlier. Twenty years ago the father strode ahead, carrying nothing; the mother followed, dragging one infant, carrying the other, and weighted down with paraphernalia. Now it was the young woman who walked ahead holding the older child by the hand, with the husband following, carrying the baby, the portable TV, the ice bucket, the sand pails and spades, the lunch boxes, the balloons, and the blow-up animals. Up and down the beach road, cutting in and out of the stalled traffic, roared young men on motorcycles picking up single girls. But lo and behold, there suddenly appeared a brigade of young women on motorbikes looking for young men to pick up.

According to Japanese folklore one is reborn on one's sixtieth birthday and starts life all over again as a baby. What then did the Empress of Japan choose as most appropriate to this uniquely Japanese tradition when she picked a gift for her husband, the Emperor, on his eightieth (i.e., second twentieth) birthday last spring: an electric razor!

(1980)

CHAPTER THIRTY-NINE

Needed: A Full-Investment Budget

ECONOMIC POLICY IN THE DEVELOPED non-Communist countries has largely been based these last thirty years on belief in John Maynard Keynes' "invisible hand": consumer demand automatically and dependably creates investment and employment. But the evidence of these thirty years—and of the New Deal policies twenty years before them—has failed to validate the Keynesian theorem. And in the last ten or fifteen years the actual experience has been the very opposite from what Keynes postulated: policies to raise consumption have produced sharply lower capital formation, declining investment, declining productivity, increasingly intractable unemployment, and self-delusions of a "soft landing."

For long years the one exception, the one non-Keynesian country, was Japan. During her years of rapid industrial growth and emergence as an economic great power Japan built her economic policy around capital formation rather than around consumption. The result was the world's highest savings rate, high investment, fast-rising productivity, high employment—and rising consumption as well. But a few years ago, largely as a result of the second "oil shock" after the Iranian Revolution of 1979, Japan too joined the parade. She is now trying to jack up consumer demand through steadily mounting deficits in the national budget—which of course is always popular in the short run, apparently painless, and thus politically tempting. Almost immediately, however, capital formation in Japan began to go down and the rate of productivity increase slowed sharply. If Japan continues on the Keynesian primrose path for a few years more, she too may become vulnerable to stagflation—the wasting disease caused by inadequate capital formation, lagging productivity, and excessive consumption.

Even the Keynesians now admit that America's greatest economic need is a rapid increase in capital formation. And all but a few Keynesian diehards—mainly to be found among politicians rather than among economists—also admit now that there is no magic wand and no Keynesian "multiplier" which automatically transforms consumer demand into capital and investment. The capital needs ahead are indeed very large and may be greater than anything we faced since the explosive industrial buildup of World War II. There is the need rapidly to automate major old industries, such as automobile-making—if it isn't done there won't be an American automobile industry ten years hence. The new growth industries—telecommunications, mini-processors, bioengineering, and so on—all require massive investment; they are all highly capital-intensive. Whichever way we tackle the energy problem— coal, "synfuels," or atomic power—capital is the basic raw material needed. And since 1950 or 1960 we have permitted transportation to erode; railroads, ports, and highways all will require billions of capital each year just to stay even.

But how can the acknowledged and persistent need for investment be built into the decision-making process and into American economic policy? The answer may well be a full-investment budget.

Twenty years ago, in the early Kennedy years, we developed the concept of the full-employment budget. Starting out from the Keynesian postulate that consumption creates investment and thus jobs, the full-employment budget calculated the amount of additional consumer demand needed to bring unemployment down to the figure theoretically considered full employment. And then, so the logic of the full-employment budget went, government deficit spending would be used to give consumers the needed extra personal income and purchasing power. Alas, the theory did not work—deficit spending created the personal income, but again and again failed to generate the promised investment.

A full-investment budget would not operate through budget deficits or budget surpluses. Its aim would mainly be not to do the wrong things—not to penalize capital formation, savings, and investment or not to subsidize excessive consumption. Its most important result, at least in the early years, would probably be identification and diagnosis: How big is the gap between the investment the American economy needs and the investment it actually receives? And what effect do certain economic, tax, and monetary policies have on capital formation? Do they encourage or discourage it?

Like the full-employment budget, the full-investment budget would start out with jobs. How many jobs does the American economy have to generate in the next three to five years, and what kinds of jobs? And then it would ask, "And how much investment is needed to provide the jobs?" For at the heart of America's investment need is the fact that the jobs for today's and tomorrow's work force require far more capital than the jobs of yesterday.

The best illustration is America's most advanced, most nearly automated, most knowledge-intensive and by far the most productive industry: agriculture. The 600,000 commercial farmers of today, who account for more than three quarters of our farm output, produce three to four times as much as the six million commercial farmers of 1940. But the capital investment per commercial farmer in 1940 was less than $35,000 in today's money. It is close to a quarter of a million today—not counting even the investment in the education of today's scientific farmer or in the sophisticated extension services, marketing services, and credit services provided to him.

In a modern manufacturing plant of today between $40,000 and $50,000 is invested in the job of a manual worker, or roughly what yesterday's commercial farmer required. The knowledge worker—the machine operator on the assembly line who moves up to being a machine programer or the technician in the automated hospital lab—needs two to three times as much investment to do his or her job. The secretary in the office works today with $3,000 worth of equipment. Her successor, the information specialist in the office of the future, will command a capital investment of close to $25,000. The productivity gains, as agriculture has proven, are likely to be very great—but this is not the main point. We have really no choice. Our labor supply will increasingly consist of people who are qualified primarily to work as knowledge workers, productive only if equipped with the tools knowledge work requires and supported by the appropriate capital investment. Eight out of every ten young people entering the labor force have finished high school—with four of them continuing school for at least another two years. A majority thus expect to do knowledge work and are, in fact, not qualified to do anything else. Whether we like it or not we will have neither productivity nor full employment unless we create jobs that fit the labor supply and make it productive. And thus a full-investment budget is the only full-employment budget that can work.

A full-investment budget is actually less innovation than adaptation. A growing number, especially of the leading companies—AT&T, for instance, or General Electric—considers investment planning the core of their strategy. These companies have learned that they will obtain the sales and profits they aim for only if they can attract and invest the appropriate capital.

Similarly we need to learn that we will not have the jobs we need unless we make the capital investment they require, but will attain our employment and productivity goals only if capital formation is adequate.

As every first-year student in economics learns, Keynes fifty years ago "repealed 'Say's Law,'" according to which savings would automatically create investment. But "Keynes' Law," which taught that consumption would automatically create investment has been proven to be even less valid. What is far more nearly true than Say's Law or Keynes' Law is that investment produces employment. Indeed everybody—whether conservative or liberal, Keynesian, Friedmanite, or "supply-sider"—accepts this by now. But we do not, so far, have a mechanism to convert this insight into policy and effective action; we do not have, so far, a full-investment budget.

(1981)

CHAPTER FORTY

A Return to Hard Choices

ACROSS WESTERN EUROPE, FROM Frankfurt and Bonn to Brussels to Oslo, the economic picture this year remains the same, regardless of changes in scenery and language: drooping productivity, unemployment especially among the young, swelling government deficits, rising inflation, and stagnating investment. "Stagflation" was the "British Sickness" ten years ago, and three years ago it was the "American Sickness." It has now become the "European Sickness."

The politicians in Europe, of course, are all blaming outside villains for their affliction. OPEC is a favorite target, even though three of Europe's sickest economies—Great Britain, the Netherlands, and Norway—are net exporters of crude oil and natural gas and therefore beneficiaries of high petroleum prices.

Only a little less popular as a villain is American economic policy with its "artificially high interest rates" and its "artificially high dollar." Only two or three years ago, however, Europeans were complaining about "artificially low U.S. interest rates" and the "artificially depressed dollar." And even the politicians admit that most of the capital outflow to the United States is not "hot money" or the short-term deposits attracted by high interest rates. Rather it consists of long-term investments, which are barely affected by interest rate differentials.

While all Western Europe suffers from the same disease, each country prescribes a sharply different therapy. The British under Mrs. Thatcher's Conservatives are engaged in the world's first experiment in monetarism. The French under Giscard d'Estaing practiced a form of supply-side economics that shifted the incidence of taxation from production to consumption.

The Germans have belatedly become Keynesians and practice "demand management"—heavy subsidies to create employment and stimulate consumption, accompanied by runaway government deficits. And now the French under their new president, Mr. Mitterrand, have made a 180-degree turn toward an even more aggressive Keynesianism than that practiced across the Rhine—complete with "pump priming," sharp wage increases and cuts in the work week, compulsory retirement with higher pensions, and soaring government spending.

Every one of these therapies is totally ineffectual.

The problem is that the Europeans still think that economic policy can be relatively painless. For the last half century, on both sides of the Atlantic, economics has been thought of as "the joyful science." However much different schools of economic thought have disagreed, they have all thought that their brand of economics could promise painless prosperity without having to face up to unpopular political choices.

Thomas Carlyle called economics the "dismal science" more than 100 years ago, because it reminds us at every turn that everything has a cost and therefore a price, that nothing can be consumed unless it has first been produced, that nothing can be produced without work and sacrifice and, above all, that we have to make choices between competing satisfactions, between today and tomorrow, and between conflicting values and goals.

The economics of the last fifty years, however, at least as understood by non-economists and politicians, have preached relatively simple and painless solutions to the problem of economic choice. The Keynesian panacea is essentially the management of consumer demand, the creation of purchasing power through government spending. The monetarist cure-all involves keeping the money supply on an even keel. For supply-side economists, cutting tax rates will simultaneously increase consumption, increase investment, *and* increase total tax revenues.

The Europeans still want to believe in these therapies. Whether their present policies are Keynesian, monetarist, or supply-side, they all express the same hope—that a country and its government need not face up to tough political decisions.

The real villains in Europe are neither OPEC nor American interest rates. Instead European policy-makers must come to grips with some difficult structural and political choices. How much national income can be transferred from producers to nonproducers? What limits are needed on the size of an economy's governmental overhead? How much national income can go into the wage fund rather than the capital fund without stimulating unemployment and depression? What rewards and incentives are needed for adequate capital formation?

These are unpopular questions. Any answer is bound to be both controversial and highly risky.

But to avoid these questions by clinging to the economics of the last fifty years may be riskier still. It is generally agreed that Mrs. Thatcher has come a cropper because she didn't face up to Britain's structural weaknesses. Relying on the panacea of monetarism, her policies left untouched the unproductive part of the British economy—an overblown government, an overpaid civil service, and heavily subsidized "losers"—while falling with full force on the productive sector. Giscard d'Estaing's version of supply-side economics had the same effect, and so does Helmut Schmidt's Keynesianism.

"Artificially high interest rates" don't explain why European capital is seeking investment in the United States; indeed they are likely to be somewhat of a deterrent. The real reason is that the Reagan administration is tackling structural problems and making choices. There is not much supply-side economics in the Reagan package; the cuts in tax rates are pretty much what any administration would have asked for at this time. But Mr. Reagan is making a genuine attempt to limit the role of government and cut back a wide range of expenditures and programs.

Whether the choices are correct is a matter of opinion. I would like to see more courage in tackling sacred cows such as Social Security and food stamps, and more discrimination in the treatment of politically weak but economically important areas such as support for science and research. But the greatest furor over the Reagan budget is not the result of the choices made; any other list would have provoked equally anguished protests. It has to do with the acceptance of reality, with the need to make choices. Economics is once again the dismal science, the science of limitations, risks, and choices.

Europe, too, will soon have to follow suit, and let economics again become "political economy." The change may not be bad for economics as a discipline. Economists, of course, would cease to be popular or friends of politicians; nobody loves a hair shirt. But economics, after all, is the discipline of rational decisions under conditions of scarcity. And such a discipline might, perhaps, be more appropriate as a conscience than a boon companion.

(1981)

The Matter of "Business Ethics"

"BUSINESS ETHICS" IS RAPIDLY becoming the "in" subject, replacing yesterday's "social responsibilities." Business ethics is now being taught in departments of philosophy, business schools, and theological seminaries. There are countless seminars on it, speeches, articles, conferences, and books, not to mention the many earnest attempts to write business ethics into the law. But what precisely is business ethics? And what could, or should, it be? Is it just another fad, and only the latest round in the hoary American blood sport of business baiting? Is there more to business ethics than the revivalist preacher's call to the sinner to repent? And if there is indeed something that one could call business ethics and could take seriously, what could it be?

Ethics is, after all, not a recent discovery. Over the centuries philosophers in their struggle with human behavior have developed different approaches to ethics, each leading to different conclusions, indeed to conflicting rules of behavior. Where does business ethics fit in—or does it fit in anywhere at all?

The confusion is so great—and the noise level even greater—that perhaps an attempt might be in order to sort out what business ethics might be, and what it might not be, in the light of the major approaches which philosophers have taken throughout the ages (though my only qualification for making this attempt is that I once, many years before anybody even thought of business ethics, taught philosophy and religion, and then worked arduously on the tangled questions of "political ethics").

Business Ethics and the Western Tradition

To the moralist of the Western tradition business ethics would make no sense. Indeed, the very term would to him be most objectionable, and reeking of moral laxity. The authorities on ethics disagreed, of course, on what constitutes the grounds of morality—whether they be divine, human nature, or the needs of society. They equally disagreed on the specific rules of ethical behavior; that sternest of moral rules, the Ten Commandments, for instance, thunders "Thou shalt not covet thy neighbor's ... maidservant." But it says nothing about sexual harassment of one's own women employees, though it was surely just as common then as now.

All authorities of the Western tradition—from the Old Testament prophets all the way to Spinoza in the seventeenth century, to Kant in the eighteenth century, Kierkegaard in the nineteenth century, and, in this century, the Englishman F. H. Bradley (*Ethical Studies*) or the American Edmond Cahn (*The Moral Decision*)—are, however, in complete agreement on one point: There is only one ethics, one set of rules of morality, one code, that of *individual* behavior in which the same rules apply to everyone alike.

A pagan could say, "Quod licet Jovi non licet bovi." He could thus hold that different rules of behavior apply to Jupiter from those that apply to the ox. A Jew or a Christian would have to reject such differentiation in ethics—and precisely because all experience shows that it always leads to exempting the "Jupiters," the great, powerful, and rich, from the rules which "the ox," the humble and poor, has to abide by.

The moralist of the Western tradition accepts "extenuating" and "aggravating" circumstances. He accepts that the poor widow who steals bread to feed her starving children deserves clemency and that it is a more heinous offense for the bishop to have a concubine than for the poor curate in the village. But before there can be extenuating or aggravating circumstances, there has to be an offense. And the offense is the same for rich and poor, for high and low alike—theft is theft, concubinage is concubinage. The reason for this insistence on a code that considers only the individual, and not his status in life or society, is precisely that otherwise the mighty, the powerful, the successful will gain exemption from the laws of ethics and morality.

The only differences between what is ethically right and ethically wrong behavior which traditional moralists, almost without exception, would accept—would indeed insist on—are differences grounded in social or cultural mores, and then only in respect to venial offenses, that is, the way things are done rather than the substance of behavior. Even in the most licentious society, fidelity to the marriage vow is meritorious, all moralists would agree; but the sexual license of an extremely permissive society, say seventeenth century Restoration England or late twentieth century America, might be considered an extenuating circumstance for the sexual transgressor. And even the sternest moralist has always insisted that, excepting only true matters of conscience, practices that are of questionable morality in one place and culture might be perfectly acceptable—and indeed might be quite ethical—in another cultural surrounding. Nepotism may be considered of dubious morality in one culture, in today's United States, for instance. In other cultures, a traditional Chinese one, for example, it may be the very essence of ethical behavior, both by satisfying the moral obligation to one's family and by making disinterested service to the public a little more likely.

But—and this is the crucial point—these are qualifications to the fundamental axiom on which the Western tradition of ethics has always been based: There is only one code of ethics, that of individual behavior, for prince and pauper, for rich and poor, for the mighty and the meek alike. Ethics, in the Judaeo-Christian tradition, is the affirmation that all men and women are alike creatures—whether the Creator be called God, Nature, or Society.

And this fundamental axiom business ethics denies. Viewed from the mainstream of traditional ethics, business ethics is not ethics at all, whatever else it may be. For it asserts that acts that are not immoral or illegal if done by ordinary folk become immoral or illegal if done by business.

One blatant example is the treatment of extortion in the current discussions of business ethics. No one ever has had a good word to say for extortion, or has advocated paying it. But if you and I are found to have paid extortion money under threat of physical or material harm, we are not considered to have behaved immorally or illegally. The extortioner is both immoral and a criminal. If a business submits to extortion, however, current business ethics considers it to have acted unethically. There is no speech, article, book, or conference on business ethics, for instance, which does not point an accusing finger in great indignation at Lockheed for giving in to a Japanese airline company, which extorted money as a prerequisite to considering the purchase of Lockheed's faltering L-1011 jet plane. There was very little difference between Lockheed's paying the Japanese and the pedestrian in New York's Central Park handing his wallet over to a mugger. Yet no one would consider the pedestrian to have acted unethically.

Similarly, in Senate confirmation hearings, one of President Reagan's cabinet appointees was accused of "unethical practices" and investigated for weeks because his New Jersey construction company was alleged to have paid money to union goons under the threat of their beating up the employees, sabotaging the trucks, and vandalizing the building sites. The accusers were self-confessed labor racketeers; no one seemed to have worried about their ethics.

One can argue that both Lockheed and the New Jersey builder were stupid to pay the holdup men. But as the old saying has it: "Stupidity is not a court martial offense." Under the new business ethics, it does become exactly that, however. And this is not compatible with what ethics always was supposed to be.

The new business ethics also denies to business the adaptation to cultural mores which has always been considered a moral duty in the traditional approach to ethics. It is now considered grossly unethical—indeed it may even be a questionable practice if not criminal offense—for an American business operating in Japan to retain as a counselor the distinguished civil servant who retires from his official position in the Japanese government. Yet the business that does not do this is considered in Japan to behave antisocially and to violate its clear ethical duties. Business taking care of retired senior civil servants, the Japanese hold, makes possible two practices they consider essential to the public interest: that a civil servant past age forty-five must retire as soon as he is out-ranked by anyone younger than he; and that governmental salaries and retirement pensions—and with them the burden of the bureaucracy on the taxpayer—be kept low, with the difference between what a first-rate man gets in government service and what he might earn in private employment made up after his retirement through his counselor's fees. The Japanese maintain that the expectation of later on being a counselor encourages a civil servant to remain incorruptible, impartial, and objective, and thus to serve only the public good; his counselorships are obtained for him by his former ministry and its recommendation depends on his rating by his colleagues as a public servant. The Germans, who follow a somewhat similar practice—with senior civil servants expected to be taken care of through appointment as industry-association executives—share this conviction. Yet, despite the fact that both the Japanese and the German systems seem to serve their respective societies well and indeed honorably, and even despite the fact that it is considered perfectly ethical for American civil servants of equal rank and caliber to move into well-paid executive jobs in business and foundations and into even more lucrative law practices, the American company in Japan that abides by a practice the Japanese consider the very essence of social responsibility, is pilloried in the present discussion of business ethics as a horrible example of unethical practices.

Surely business ethics assumes that for some reason the ordinary rules of ethics do not apply to business. Business ethics, in other words, is not ethics at all, as the term has commonly been used by Western philosophers and Western theologians. What is it then?

Casuistry: The Ethics of Social Responsibility

"It's casuistry," the historian of Western philosophy would answer. Casuistry asserted that rulers, because of their responsibility, have to strike a balance between the ordinary demands of ethics which apply to them as individuals and their social responsibility to their subjects, their kingdom—or their company.

Casuistry was first propounded in Calvin's *Institutes*, then taken over by the Catholic theologians of the Counter-Reformation (Bellarmin, for instance, or St. Charles Borromeus) and developed into a political ethic by their Jesuit disciples in the seventeenth century.

Casuistry was the first attempt to think through social responsibility and to embed it in a set of special ethics for those in power. In this respect, business ethics tries to do exactly what the casuists did 300 years ago. And it must end the same way. If business ethics continues to be casuistry its speedy demise in a cloud of ill-repute can be confidently predicted.

To the casuist the social responsibility inherent in being a ruler—that is, someone whose actions have impact on others—is by itself an ethical imperative. As such, the ruler has a duty, as Calvin first laid down, to subordinate his individual behavior and his individual conscience to the demands of his social responsibility.

The *locus classicus* of casuistry is Henry VIII and his first marriage to Catherine of Aragon. A consummated marriage—and Catherine of Aragon had a daughter by Henry, the future "Bloody Mary"— could not be dissolved except by death, both Catholic and Protestant theologians agreed. In casuistry, however, as both Catholics and Protestants agreed, Henry VIII had an ethical duty to seek annulment of the marriage. Until his father, well within living memory, had snatched the Crown by force of arms, England had suffered a century of bloody and destructive civil war because of the lack of a legitimate male heir. Without annulment of his marriage, Henry VIII, in other words, exposed his country and its people to mortal danger, well beyond anything he could in conscience justify. The one point on which Protestants and Catholics disagreed was whether the Pope also had a social, and thereby an ethical, responsibility to grant Henry's request. By not granting it, he drove the King and his English subjects out of the Catholic Church. But had he granted the annulment, the Catholic casuists argued, the Pope would have driven Catherine's uncle, the Holy Roman Emperor, out of the Church and into the waiting arms of an emerging Protestantism; and that would have meant that instead of assigning a few million Englishmen to heresy, perdition, and hellfire, many times more souls—all the people in all the lands controlled by the Emperor, that is, in most of Europe—could have been consigned to everlasting perdition.

This may be considered a quaint example—but only because our time judges behavior by economic rather than theological absolutes. The example illustrates what is wrong with casuistry and indeed why it must fail as an approach to ethics. In the first place casuistry must end up becoming politicized, precisely because it considers social responsibility an ethical absolute. In giving primacy to political values and goals it subordinates ethics to politics. Clearly this is the approach business ethics today is taking. Its very origin is in politics rather than in ethics. It expresses a belief that the responsibility which business and the business executive have, precisely because they have social impact, must determine ethics—and this is a political rather than an ethical imperative.

Equally important, the casuist inevitably becomes the apologist for the ruler, the powerful. Casuistry starts out with the insight that the behavior of rulers affects more than themselves and their families. It thus starts out by making demands on the ruler—the starting point for both Calvin and his Catholic disciples in the Counter-Reformation fifty years later. It then concludes that rulers must, therefore, in conscience and ethics, subordinate their interests, including their individual morality, to their social responsibility. But this implies that the rules which decide what is ethical for ordinary people do not apply equally, if at all, to those with social responsibility. Ethics for them is instead a cost-benefit calculation involving the demands of individual conscience and the demands of position—and that means that the rulers are exempt from the demands of ethics, if only their behavior can be argued to confer benefits on other people. And this is precisely how business ethics is going.

Indeed, under casuist analysis the ethical violations which to most present proponents of business ethics appear the most heinous crimes turn out to have been practically saintly.

Take Lockheed's bribe story for instance. Lockheed was led into paying extortion money to a Japanese airline by the collapse of the supplier of the engines for its wide-bodied L-1011 passenger jet, the English Rolls Royce Company. At that time Lockheed employed some 25,000 people making L-1011s, most of them in southern California which then, 1972–73, was suffering substantial unemployment from sharp cutbacks in defense orders in the aerospace industry. To safeguard the 25,000 jobs, Lockheed got a large government subsidy. But to be able to maintain these jobs, Lockheed needed at least one large L-1011 order from one major airline. The only one among the major airlines not then committed to a competitor's plane was All-Nippon Airways in Japan. The self-interest of

Lockheed Corporation and of its stockholders would clearly have demanded speedy abandonment of the L-1011. It was certain that it would never make money—and it has not made a penny yet. Jettisoning the L-1011 would immediately have boosted Lockheed's earnings, maybe doubled them. It would have immediately boosted Lockheed's share price; stock market analysts and investment bankers pleaded with the firm to get rid of the albatross. If Lockheed had abandoned the L-1011, instead of paying extortion money to the Japanese for ordering a few planes and thus keeping the project alive, the company's earnings, its stock price, and the bonuses and stock options of top management, would immediately have risen sharply. Not to have paid extortion money to the Japanese would to a casuist, have been self-serving. To a casuist, paying the extortion money was a duty and social responsibility to which the self-interest of the company, its shareholders, and its executives had to be subordinated. It was the discharge of social responsibility of the ruler to keep alive the jobs of 25,000 people at a time when jobs in the aircraft industry in southern California were scarce indeed.

Similarly, the other great horror story of business ethics would, to the casuist, appear as an example of business virtue if not of unselfish business martyrdom. In the "electrical apparatus conspiracy" of the late 1950s, several high-ranking General Electric executives were sent to jail. They were found guilty of a criminal conspiracy in violation of antitrust because orders for heavy generating equipment, such as turbines, were parceled out among the three electrical apparatus manufacturers in the United States—General Electric, Westinghouse, and Allis Chalmers. But this "criminal conspiracy" only served to reduce General Electric's sales, its profits, and the bonuses and stock options of the General Electric executives who took part in the conspiracy. Since the electric apparatus cartel was destroyed by the criminal prosecution of the General Electric executives, General Electric sales and profits in the heavy apparatus field have sharply increased, as has market penetration by the company, which now has what amounts to a near-monopoly. The purpose of the cartel—which incidentally was started under federal government pressure in the Depression years to fight unemployment—was the protection of the weakest and most dependent of the companies, Allis Chalmers (which is located in Milwaukee, a depressed and declining old industrial area). As soon as government action destroyed the cartel, Allis Chalmers had to go out of the turbine business and had to lay off several thousand people. And while there is still abundant competition in the world market for heavy electric apparatus, General Electric now enjoys such market dominance in the home market that the United States, in case of war, would not have major alternative suppliers of so critical a product as turbines.

The casuist would agree that cartels are both illegal and considered immoral in the United States—although not necessarily anyplace else in the world. But he would also argue that the General Electric executive who violated U.S. law had an ethical duty to do so under the higher law of social responsibility to safeguard both employment in the Milwaukee area and the defense-production base of the United States.

The only thing that is surprising about these examples is that business has not yet used them to climb on the casuist bandwagon of business ethics. For just as almost any behavior indulged in by the seventeenth century ruler could be shown to be an ethical duty by the seventeenth century disciples of Calvin, of Bellarmin, and of Borromeus, so almost any behavior of the executive in organizations today—whether in a business, a hospital, a university, or a government agency—could be shown to be his ethical duty under the casuistic cost-benefit analysis between individual ethics and the demands of social responsibility. There are indeed signs aplenty that that most apolitical of rulers, the American business executive, is waking up to the political potential of business ethics. Some of the advertisements which large companies—Mobil Oil, for example—are now running to counter the attacks made on them in the name of social responsibility and business ethics, clearly use the casuist approach to defend business, and indeed to counterattack. But if business ethics becomes a tool to defend as ethical acts on the part of executives that would be condemned if committed by anyone else, the present proponents of business ethics, like their casuist predecessors 400 years ago, will have no one to blame but themselves.

Casuistry started out as high morality. In the end, its ethics came to be summed up in two well-known pieces of cynicism: "An ambassador is an honest man, lying abroad for the good of his country," went a well-known eighteenth century pun. And a hundred years later, Bismarck said, "What a scoundrel a minister would be if, in his own private life, he did half the things he has a duty to do to be true to his oath of office."

Long before that, however, casuistry had been killed off by moral revulsion. Its most lasting memories perhaps are the reactions to it which re-established ethics in the West as a universal system, binding the individual regardless of station, function, or social responsibility: Spinoza's *Ethics*, and the *Provincial Letters* of his contemporary, Blaise Pascal. But also—and this is a lesson that might be pondered by today's proponents of business ethics, so many of whom are clergymen—it was their embracing casuistry that made the Jesuits hated and despised, made "Jesuitical" a synonym of immoral, and led to the Jesuit order being suppressed by the Pope in the eighteenth century. And it is casuistry, more than anything else, that has caused the anticlericalism of the intellectuals in Catholic Europe.

Business ethics undoubtedly is a close parallel to casuistry. Its origin is political, as was that of casuistry. Its basic thesis, that ethics for the ruler, and especially for the business executive, has to express social responsibility is exactly the starting point of the casuist. But if business ethics is casuistry, then it will not last long—and long before it dies, it will have become a tool of the business executive to justify what for other people would be unethical behavior, rather than a tool to restrain the business executive and to impose tight ethical limits on business.

The Ethics of Prudence and Self-Development

There is one other major tradition of ethics in the West, the Ethics of Prudence. It goes all the way back to Aristotle and his enthrone-ment of prudence as a cardinal virtue. It continued for almost 2,000 years in the popular literary tradition of the "Education of the Christian Prince," which reached its ultimate triumph and its reduc-tion to absurdity in Machiavelli's *Prince*. Its spirit can best be summed up by the advice which then-Senator Harry Truman gave to an Army witness before his committee in the early years of World War II: "Generals should never do anything that needs to be explained to a Senate Committee—there is nothing one can explain to a Senate Committee."

"Generals," whether the organization is an army, a corporation, or a university, are highly visible. They must expect their behavior to be seen, scrutinized, analyzed, discussed, and questioned. Pru-dence thus demands that they shun actions that cannot easily be understood, explained, or justified. But generals, being visible, are also examples. They are leaders by their very position and visibility. Their only choice is whether their example leads others to right action or to wrong action. Their only choice is between direction and misdirection, between leadership and misleadership. They thus have an ethical obligation to give the example of right behavior and to avoid giving the example of wrong behavior.

The Ethics of Prudence does not spell out what "right" behavior is. They assume that what is wrong behavior is clear enough—and if there is any doubt, it is "questionable" and to be avoided. Pru-dence makes it an ethical duty for the leader to exemplify the pre-cepts of ethics in his own behavior.

And by following prudence, everyone regardless of status becomes a leader, a superior man and will "fulfill himself," to use the contemporary idiom. One becomes the superior man by avoid-ing any act which would make one the kind of person one does not want to be, does not respect, does not accept as superior. "If you don't want to see a pimp when you look in the shaving mirror in the morning, don't hire call girls the night before to entertain congressmen, customers, or salesmen." On any other basis, hiring call girls may be condemned as vulgar and tasteless, and may be shunned as something fastidious people do not do. It may be frowned upon as uncouth. It may even be illegal. But only in prudence is it ethically relevant. This is what Kierkegaard, the sternest moralist of the nineteenth century, meant when he said that aesthetics is the true ethics.

The Ethics of Prudence can easily degenerate. Concern with what one can justify becomes, only too easily, concern with appearances—Machiavelli was by no means the first to point out that in a Prince, that is, in someone with authority and high visibility, appearances may matter more than substance. The Ethics of Prudence thus easily decays into the hypocrisy of public relations. Leadership through right example easily degenerates into the sham of charisma and into a cloak for misdirection and misleadership—it is always the Hitlers and the Stalins who are the great charismatic leaders. And fulfilment through self-development into a superior person—what Kierkegaard called "becoming a Christian"—may turn either into the smugness of the Pharisee who thanks God that he is not like other people, or into self-indulgence instead of self-discipline, moral sloth instead of self-respect, and into saying "I like," rather than "I know."

Yet, despite these degenerative tendencies, the Ethics of Prudence is surely appropriate to a society of organizations. Of course, it will not be business ethics—it makes absolutely no difference in the Ethics of Prudence whether the executive is a general in the Army, a bureau chief in the Treasury Department in Washington, a senator, a judge, a senior vice president in a bank, or a hospital administrator. But a society of organizations is a society in which an extraordinarily large number of people are in positions of high visibility, if only within one organization. They enjoy this visibility not, like the Christian Prince, by virtue of birth, nor by virtue of wealth—that is, not because they are personages. They are functionaries and important only through their responsibility to take right action. But this is exactly what the Ethics of Prudence is all about.

Similarly, executives set examples, whatever the organization. They set the tone, create the spirit, decide the values for an organization and for the people in it. They lead or mislead, in other words. And they have no choice but to do one or the other. Above all, the ethics or aesthetics of self-development would seem to be tailor-made for the specific dilemma of the executive in the modern organization. By himself he is a nobody and indeed anonymous. A week after he has retired and has left that big corner office on the twenty-sixth floor of his company's skyscraper or the Secretary's six-room corner suite on Constitution Avenue, no one in the building even recognizes him anymore. And his neighbors in the pleasant suburb in which he lives in a comfortable middle-class house—very different from anything one might call a palace—only know that "Joe works someplace on Park Avenue" or "does something in the government." Yet collectively these anonymous executives are the leaders in a modern society. Their function demands the self-discipline and the self-respect of the superior man. To live up to the performance expectations society makes upon them, they have to strive for self-fulfilment rather than be content with lackadaisical mediocrity. Yet at the pinnacle of their career and success, they are still cogs in an organization and easily replaceable. And this is exactly what self-fulfilment in ethics, the Kierkegaardian "becoming a Christian," concerns itself with: how to become the superior man, important and autonomous, without being a big shot let alone a Prince.

One would therefore expect the discussion of business ethics to focus on the Ethics of Prudence. Some of the words, such as to "fulfill oneself," indeed sound the same, though they mean something quite different. But by and large, the discussion of business ethics, even if more sensibly concerning itself with the ethics of organization, will have nothing to do with prudence.

The reason is clearly that the Ethics of Prudence is the ethics of authority. And while today's discussion of business ethics (or of the ethics of university administration, of hospital administration, or of government) clamors for responsibility, it rejects out of hand any authority and, of course, particularly any authority of the business executive. Authority is not legitimate; it is "elitism." But there can be no responsibility where authority is denied. To deny it is not anarchism nor radicalism, let alone socialism. In a child, it is called a temper tantrum.

The Ethics of Interdependence

Casuistry was so thoroughly discredited that the only mention of it to be found in most textbooks on the history of philosophy is in connection with its ultimate adversaries—Spinoza and Pascal. Indeed, only ten or fifteen years ago, few if any philosophers would have thought it possible for anything like "business ethics" to emerge. "Particularist ethics," a set of ethics that postulates that this or that group is different in its ethical responsibilities from everyone else, would have been considered doomed forever by the failure of casuistry. Ethics, almost anyone in the West would have considered axiomatic, would surely always be ethics of the individual and independent of rank and station.

But there is another, non-Western ethics that is situational. It is the most successful and most durable ethics of them all: the Confucian ethics of interdependence.

Confucian ethics elegantly sidesteps the trap into which the casuists fell; it is a universal ethics, in which the same rules and imperatives of behavior hold for every individual. There is no social responsibility overriding individual conscience, no cost-benefit calculation, no greater good or higher measure than the individual and his behavior, and altogether no casuistry. In the Confucian ethics, the rules are the same for all. But there are different general rules, according to the five basic relationships of interdependence, which for the Confucian embrace the totality of individual interactions in civil society: superior and subordinate (or master and servant); father and child; husband and wife; oldest brother and sibling; friend and friend. Right behavior—what in the English translation of Confucian ethics is usually called "sincerity"*—is that individual behavior which is truly appropriate to the specific relationship of mutual dependence because it optimizes benefits for both parties. Other behavior is insincere and therefore wrong behavior and unethical. It creates dissonance instead of harmony, exploitation instead of benefits, manipulation instead of trust.

An example of the Confucian approach to the ethical problems discussed under the heading of business ethics would be sexual harassment. To the Confucian it is clearly unethical behavior because it injects power into a relationship that is based on function. This makes it exploitation. That this insincere—that is, grossly unethical—behavior on the part of a superior takes place within a business or any other kind of organization, is basically irrelevant. The master/servant or superior/subordinate relationship is one between individuals. Hence, the Confucian would make no distinction between a general manager forcing his secretary into sexual intercourse and Mr. Samuel Pepys, England's famous seventeenth century diarist, forcing his wife's maids to submit to his amorous advances. It would not even make much difference to the Confucian that today's secretary can, as a rule, quit without suffering more than inconvenience if she does not want to submit, whereas the poor wretches in Mrs. Pepys' employ ended up as prostitutes, either because they did not submit and were fired and out on the

* No word has caused more misunderstanding in East/West relations than "sincerity." To a Westerner, sincerity means "words that are true to conviction and feelings"; to an Easterner, sincerity means "actions that are appropriate to a specific relationship and make it harmonious and of optimum mutual benefit." For the Westerner, sincerity has to do with intentions, that is, with morality; to the Easterner, sincerity has to do with behavior, that is, with ethics.

street, or because they did submit and were fired when they got pregnant. Nor would the Confucian see much difference between a corporation vice president engaging in sexual harassment and a college professor seducing coeds with implied promises to raise their grades.

And finally, it would be immaterial to the Confucian that the particular insincerity involves sexual relations. The superior would be equally guilty of grossly unethical behavior and violation of fundamental rules of conduct if, as a good many of the proponents of business ethics ardently advocate, he were to set himself up as a mental therapist for his subordinates and help them to adjust. No matter how benevolent his intentions, this is equally incompatible with the integrity of the superior/subordinate relationship. It equally abuses rank based on function and imposes power. It is therefore exploitation whether done because of lust for power or manipulation or done out of benevolence—either way it is unethical and destructive. Both sexual relations and the healer/patient relationship must be free of rank to be effective, harmonious, and ethically correct. They are constructive only as friend to friend or as husband to wife relations, in which differences in function confer no rank whatever.

This example makes it clear, I would say, that virtually all the concerns of business ethics, indeed almost everything business ethics considers a problem, have to do with relationships of interdependence, whether that between the organization and the employee, the manufacturer and the customer, the hospital and the patient, the university and the student, and so on.

Looking at the ethics of interdependence immediately resolves the conundrum which confounds the present discussion of business ethics: What difference does it make whether a certain act or behavior takes place in a business, in a non-profit organization, or outside any organization at all? The answer is clear: none at all. Indeed the questions that are so hotly debated in today's discussion of business ethics, such as whether changing a hospital from "non-profit" to "proprietary and for profit" will affect either its behavior or the ethics pertaining to it, the most cursory exposure to the ethics of interdependence reveals as sophistry and as nonquestions.

The ethics of interdependence thus does address itself to the question which business ethics tries to tackle. But today's discussion, explicitly or implicitly, denies the basic insight from which the ethics of interdependence starts and to which it owes its strength and durability: It denies *interdependence*.

The ethics of interdependence, as Confucian philosophers first codified it shortly after their Master's death in 479 B.C., considers illegitimate and unethical the injection of power into human relationships. It asserts that interdependence demands equality of obligations. Children owe obedience and respect to their parents. Parents, in turn, owe affection, sustenance and, yes, respect, to their children. For every paragon of filial piety in Confucian hagiology, such as the dutiful daughter, there is a paragon of parental sacrifice, such as the loving father who sacrificed his brilliant career at the court to the care of his five children and their demands on his time and attention. For every minister who risks his job, if not his life, by fearlessly correcting an Emperor guilty of violating harmony, there is an Emperor laying down his life rather than throw a loyal minister to the political wolves.

In the ethics of interdependence there are only obligations, and all obligations are mutual obligations. Harmony and trust—that is, interdependence—require that each side be obligated to provide what the other side needs to achieve its goals and to fulfill itself.

But in today's American—and European—discussion of business ethics, ethics means that one side has obligations and the other side has rights, if not entitlements. This is not compatible with the ethics of interdependence and indeed with any ethics at all. It is the politics of power, and indeed the politics of naked exploitation and repression. And within the context of interdependence the exploiters and the oppressors are not the bosses, but the ones who assert their rights rather than accept mutual obligation, and with it, equality.

To redress the balance in a relationship of interdependence—or at least so the ethics of interdependence would insist—demands not pitting power against power or right against right, but matching obligation to obligation.

To illustrate: Today's ethics of organization debate pays great attention to the duty to be a "whistle-blower" and to the protection of the whistle-blower against retaliation or suppression by his boss or by his organization. This sounds high-minded. Surely, the subordinate has a right, if not indeed a duty, to bring to public attention and remedial action his superior's misdeeds, let alone violation of the law on the part of a superior or of his employing organization. But in the context of the ethics of interdependence, whistle-blowing is ethically quite ambiguous. To be sure, there are misdeeds of the superior or of the employing organization which so grossly violate propriety and laws that the subordinate (or the friend, or the child, or even the wife) cannot remain silent. This is, after all, what the word "felony" implies; one becomes a partner to a felony and criminally liable by not reporting, and thus compounding it. But otherwise? It is not primarily that to encourage whistle-blowing corrodes the bond of trust that ties the superior to the subordinate. Encouraging the whistle-blower must make the subordinate lose his trust in the superior's willingness and ability to protect his people. They simply are no longer his people and become potential enemies or political pawns. And in the end, encouraging and indeed even permitting whistle-blowers always makes the weaker one—that is, the subordinate—powerless against the unscrupulous superior, simply because the superior no longer can recognize or meet his obligation to the subordinate.

Whistle-blowing, after all, is simply another word for informing. And perhaps it is not quite irrelevant that the only societies in Western history that encouraged informers were bloody and infamous tyrannies—Tiberius and Nero in Rome, the Inquisition in the Spain of Philip II, the French Terror, and Stalin. It may also be no accident that Mao, when he tried to establish a dictatorship in China, organized whistle-blowing on a massive scale. For under whistle-blowing, under the regime of the informer, no mutual trust, no interdependencies, and no ethics are possible. And Mao only followed history's first totalitarians, the "Legalists" of the third century B.C., who suppressed Confucius and burned his books because he had taught ethics and had rejected the absolutism of political power.

The limits of mutual obligation are indeed a central and difficult issue in the ethics of interdependencies. But to start out, as the advocates of whistle-blowing do, with the assumption that there are only rights on one side, makes any ethics impossible. And if the fundamental problem of ethics is the behavior in relations of interdependence, then obligations have to be mutual and have to be equal for both sides. Indeed, in a relationship of interdependence it is the mutuality of obligation that creates true equality, regardless of differences in rank, wealth, or power.

Today's discussion of business ethics stridently denies this. It tends to assert that in relations of interdependence one side has all the duties and the other one all the rights. But this is the assertion of the Legalist, the assertion of the totalitarians who shortly end up by denying all ethics. It must also mean that ethics becomes the tool of the powerful. If a set of ethics is one-sided, then the rules are written by those that have the position, the power, the wealth. If interdependence is not equality of obligations, it becomes domination.

Looking at business ethics as an ethics of interdependence reveals an additional and equally serious problem—indeed a *more* serious problem.

Can an ethics of interdependence be anything more than ethics for individuals? The Confucians said no—a main reason why Mao outlawed them. For the Confucian—but also for the philosopher of the Western tradition—only *law* can handle the rights and objections of collectives. *Ethics* is always a matter of the person.

But is this adequate for a society of organizations such as ours? This may be the central question for the philosopher of modern society, in which access to livelihood, career, and achievement exist primarily in and through organizations—and especially for the highly educated person for whom opportunities outside of organizations are very scarce indeed. In such a society, both the society and the individual increasingly depend on the performance, as well as the sincerity, of organizations.

But in today's discussion of business ethics it is not even seen that there is a problem.

"Ethical Chic" or Ethics

Business ethics, this discussion should have made clear, is to ethics what soft porn is to the Platonic Eros; soft porn too talks of something it calls "love." And insofar as business ethics comes even close to ethics, it comes close to casuistry and will, predictably, end up as a fig leaf for the shameless and as special pleading for the powerful and the wealthy.

Clearly, one major element of the peculiar stew that goes by the name of business ethics is plain old-fashioned hostility to business and to economic activity altogether—one of the oldest of American traditions and perhaps the only still-potent ingredient in the Puritan heritage. Otherwise, we would not even talk of business ethics. There is no warrant in any ethics to consider one major sphere of activity as having its own ethical problems, let alone its own ethics. Business or economic activity may have special political or legal dimensions as in "business and government," to cite the title of a once-popular college course, or as in the antitrust laws. And business ethics may be good politics or good electioneering. But that is all. For ethics deals with the right actions of individuals. And then it surely makes no difference whether the setting is a community hospital, with the actors a nursing supervisor and the consumer a patient, or whether the setting is National Universal General Corporation, the actors a quality control manager, and the consumer the buyer of a bicycle.

But one explanation for the popularity of business ethics is surely also the human frailty of which Pascal accused the casuists of his day: the lust for power and prominence of a clerisy sworn to humility. Business ethics is fashionable, and provides speeches at conferences, lecture fees, consulting assignments, and lots of publicity. And surely business ethics, with its tales of wrongdoing in high places, caters also to the age-old enjoyment of society gossip and to the prurience which—it was, I believe, Rabelais who said it—makes it fornication when a peasant has a toss in the hay and romance when the prince does it.

Altogether, business ethics might well be called ethical chic rather than ethics—and indeed might be considered more a media event than philosophy or morals.

But this discussion of the major approaches to ethics and of their concerns surely also shows that ethics has as much to say to the individual in our society of organizations as they ever had to say to the individual in earlier societies. They are just as important and just as needed nowadays. And they surely require hard and serious work.

A society of organizations is a society of interdependence. The specific relationship which the Confucian philosopher postulated as universal and basic may not be adequate, or even appropriate, to modern society and to the ethical problems within the modern organization and between the modern organization and its clients, customers, and constituents. But the fundamental concepts surely are. Indeed, if there ever is a viable ethics of organization, it will almost certainly have to adopt the key concepts which have made Confucian ethics both durable and effective:

- Clear definition of the fundamental relationships;

- Universal and general rules of conduct—that is, rules that are binding on any one person or organization, according to its rules, function, and relationships;

- Focus on right behavior rather than on avoiding wrongdoing, and on behavior rather than on motives or intentions. And finally,

- An effective organization ethic, indeed an organization ethic that deserves to be seriously considered as ethics, will have to define right behavior as the behavior which optimizes each party's benefits and thus makes the relationship harmonious, constructive, and mutually beneficial.

But a society of organizations is also a society in which a great many people are unimportant and indeed anonymous by themselves, yet are highly visible, and matter as leaders in society. And thus it is a society that must stress the Ethics of Prudence and self-development. It must expect its managers, executives, and professionals to demand of themselves that they shun behavior they would not respect in others, and instead practice behavior appropriate to the sort of person they would want to see in the mirror in the morning.

(1981)

ACKNOWLEDGMENTS

This volume owes its conception and birth to Truman M. Talley, its publisher. Mr. Talley first suggested putting together a selection of my *Wall Street Journal* articles that merited book publication. He then cheerfully tackled the task of selecting the pieces that remained useful and timely and therefore warranted being put between book covers. And he patiently and with never-failing good humor pushed and pushed and pushed again to get me to tie together and finish the necessary work. This book and I owe him a great deal.

I also owe especial thanks to my old friend and literary agent, John Cushman, who acted as editorial conscience and adviser to Mr. Talley and myself.

Thanks are due also to the *Wall Street Journal*, to the *Journal's* brilliant Editor, Robert Bartley, and to Tom Bray and Adam Meyerson of the editorial page—for encouragement, for advice and criticism, for friendly but firm editing, and for permission to reprint these articles in book form.

In preparing the book chapters from the original articles I have made the minimum of changes. In a few cases I have taken out references to books or articles. I have clarified time references. When an article written in the spring of 1980 talked, for instance, of "the forthcoming election," I have changed this to read "the election in the fall of 1980." When an article written in 1977 said "next year," I have put in, instead, "1978." In a few cases I have shortened or altered a former chapter title that seemed to me to be unduly ponderous. But I have refrained from rewriting and from putting hindsight to work. Readers will therefore be able to judge for themselves how often and where the author was right and how often and where he was dead wrong.

INDEX

book publishing, size versus profitability in, 85
Boston Consulting Group, 85
Brazil, 183
Bretton Woods Conference, 211
British National Health Service, 128
budgets. *See also* capital investment and structure
    full-employment, 220
    full-investment, 219–222
    short- versus long-term, 42–43
Bullock Report, British Royal Commission, 195
business. *See also* companies
    destructive "rational" policies of, 5
    growth as hazard for, 14
    inflation-proofing of, 3–7
    long-term policies as essential to, 6
    public's economic illiteracy about, 47
business ethics, 227–249
    authority versus responsibility in, 241
    cartels and, 235–236
    casuistry versus, 232–238
    as "chic," 247–248
    Confucian ethics (relationships of interdependence) and, 242–247, 248–249
    cost-benefit mentality and, 234, 236
    extortion and, 230–231, 234–235
    hostility to business and, 247
    model role of executives in, 240
    organization ethic and, 241, 245, 247, 248–249
    Prudence Ethic and, 238–241, 249
    sexual harassment and, 228, 242–243
    social-cultural mores and, 231–232
    traditional ethics versus, 230, 232
    in Western tradition, 228–232
    whistle-blowing and, 245–246
business growth. *See also* speculative growth
    concentration needed for, 17, 87
    desirable versus undesirable, 57, 85, 88
    as "different" versus "more," 16
    distortions of inflation and, 88
    exploitation of opportunity for, 87
    five rules in management of, 14–19
    goals for, 86, 88
    marginal status and, 85–86
    need in near future for, 56–57
    "obesity" versus, 85, 88
    policy for, 85, 87–88
    provisions for, as capital charge, 75
    realistic appraisals and, 18
    risk period following, 75
    speculative, aftermath of, 53–60
    strategy for, 85, 86–88

    volume versus, 88
    what to abandon for, 18, 87–88
    in zero growth years, 89
business travel, 81
    information technology and, 36–37

Cahn, Edmond, 228
California, retirement law in, 27
Calvin, John, 232, 233, 234
capital
    changes in supply sources of, 54–55
    cost of, 48, 50, 65, 74, 75–76
    fixed human, 66
    "genuine" savings and, 71
capital charges, in earnings-per-share measure, 75–77
capital formation
    full-investment budgeting and, 220–222
    income distribution versus, 59
    industrial growth and, 220–222
    in Keynesian theory, 218–219, 220
    labor-income ratio and, 95, 96–97, 98–99
    myths about, 72–73
    savings in, 70
capital investment and structure
    after go-go era, 54
    board of directors' role in, 33
    as core strategy, 221
    in creation of jobs, 50, 54, 220–221
    feedback on, 63, 65
    by foreign managers, 43
    growth of business and, 14–15
    in inflationary period, 5
    in management audit, 9–10
    managing productivity of, 61–67
    meaningful components in, 63–64
    for rapid growth, 15–16
    Rostow thesis and, 205
    rules for managing productivity and, 64–66
capitalism
    job as property right and, 177
    Marx's view of, 61, 62
    profit and, 51
CARE, 106
Carlyle, Thomas, 224
cartels, business ethics and, 235–236
Carter, Jimmy, 114, 118, 120, 124, 209
cash flow, emphasis on, 54, 56
casuistry
    as apology for power, 234
    business ethics versus, 232–238
    as discredited, 237, 241
    political nature of, 234
catastrophic-illness insurance, 125–126

China, People's Republic of, 59, 92, 203
    Japanese exports to, 192, 200, 201
Chrysler Corporation, 86, 168, 170, 195
churches, role of, 106
co-determination issue, 194–196
    disenfranchisement of managers and,
        195–195
    political aspects of, 194, 195
college recruiting, 166
Common Market
    production sharing in, 182
    U.S. export surplus with, 96
Communist economies
    downward capital productivity in, 62
    profit and, 51
companies. *See also* executives
    audit committee of independent directors
        in, 31, 35
    board of directors' role in (*See* boards of
        directors)
    mandatory audits and, 9
    pension funds as controlling element in, 177
    in wrong business, 13, 33
computers, changes caused by, 37–39
Confucian ethics of interdependence, 242–247
    appropriateness for modern society of,
        248–249
    five basic relationships in, 242
    Legalists and, 246
    obligation versus power in, 244–246
    "sincerity" in, 242
consumer demand
    capital investment and, 54
    economic activity linked to, 68–69
    employment rate and, 158–159
    explanations of, 80–84
    for health-care services, 124, 128
    Keynesian theory and, 218–219, 220, 222,
        224, 225
    of married working women, 83–84
    of retired people, 82–83
    of young adults, 83
consumer market
    historical changes in, 84
    new segmentation of, 82–84
corporation income tax, as regressive, 71–72
"cost of capital," 48
costs
    capital charges as, 75–76
    profits versus, 49–52
counselors, post-retirement executives as,
        28–29
credit
    capital management policies and, 65–66
    crunches, 4, 6

currencies, 207–212. *See also* transnational
        currencies
    political aspects of, 210, 211–212
    two-tier structure for, 207–208, 212
    U.S. dollar, 208, 210, 211, 223
cyclical earnings, 77

deficiency of revenue, as capital charge, 75
deficits, government, 55, 219, 220, 224
"demand-management," 179
    in Keynesian theory, 218–222, 224, 225
demography, 156
    baby boom problem and, 164–167
    consumer demand and, 68–69
    growth planning and, 87
    labor supply and, 51, 54, 66–69, 91–92, 121,
        142, 144, 150–151, 169, 182–183,
        187–190, 221
    re-industrialization and, 91–92, 92–93, 94
    school enrollments and, 135
    Social Security program and, 117
    world economy and, 121, 169–170, 180,
        182–183
dental insurance plans, 126
developed countries
    downward capital productivity in, 62
    job as property right in, 174–177
    Keynesian investment theory in,
        218–219, 222
    obsolete economic policies in, 179
    re-industrialization in, 91–93
    unionism versus production sharing in,
        122, 170, 184
developing countries
    appropriate technologies for, 202–206
    capital investment theory in, 205
    demographic shifts in, 91–92
    Japanese exports to, 192, 193
    production sharing and, 122, 169–170,
        182–184
    "smallness" rhetoric in, 203, 205–206
    unskilled workers in, 39, 92, 182–183
DuPont Company, 44, 77

earnings per share
    capital charges and, 75–77
    as measure of performance, 55–56, 74–79
    as misnomer, 75
    "taxable earnings" versus, 75
economic myths, 68–73
    capital formation and, 72–73
    on corporation income tax, 71–72
    on income distribution, 72
    on nature of consumer demand, 68–69,
        80–81

satellite transmission, for business
    subscribers, 37
Saudi Arabia, 192
savings, 87
    capital formation and, 71
    stagflation and, 82
    of wage earners, 98
Say's Law, 222
Schmidt, Helmut, 225
school system, 135–139. *See also* universities
    continuing professional education and,
        136–137, 138
    demographic factors in, 135
    diversity of teaching approaches required
        in, 137–138
    fundamentalist and evangelical schools
        in, 139
    humanities displaced in, 137
    near-future objectives of, 136–138
    social changes and, 135–136
    "voucher" system in, 138
Schumpeter, Joseph, 61
Seattle Art Museum, 104
second careers, 29, 133, 147, 153
Securities and Exchange Commission, 31, 184
shoe workers, 121–122
Siemens, 6
Simons, Henry, 98
Singapore, 181
Sloan, Alfred, 84
Smith, Adam, 98
social policies
    changes toward age and gender in, 144–149
    on displaced workers, 121
    government bureaucracies and, 117–118
    managerial policies and, 43
    nineteenth-century, 143
    profit linked to responsibility in, 52
social responsibility, casuistry and, 232–238
Social Security program, 117, 145–146, 151,
        152, 226
Solomon, Ezra, 48
Sony Corporation, 199
South Korea, 122, 169, 181
Soviet Union, 62, 201, 208
Spain, 174
speculative growth
    aftermath of, 53–60
    structural changes in economy and,
        54–56
    world economy and, 57–59
Spinoza, B., 237
Stages of Economic Growth, The (Rostow), 205
stages of production process, 121, 169,
        181–182, 183

stagflation, 219
    consumer response and, 81–82
steel industry, 120, 121, 168, 170, 203, 204
    labor-income ratio in, 95, 96, 97–98
Stigler, George, 98
Stinnes, Hugo, 5
stock market, valuation criteria of, 78–79
stock options, executives' income and,
        21–22, 56
student-exchange programs, 106
sunset laws, 118
supply-side economics, 222, 224, 225, 226
surplus, as "profit," 48
Sweden, 120, 128, 172, 185
systems approach, for multinationals, 185

taxes, tax policies
    executives' shelters and, 21
    gimmicks, 21–22
    indexing compensation and, 122–123
    money versus real income and, 20–21
    myths about, 71–72
    reform, union and business agreement
        on, 23
    stimulation of capital formation and, 193
technological changes, 37–39. *See also*
        information technology; knowledge
        workers
    appropriateness of, 202–206
    class of '68 and, 155–156
    jobs and, 170
    re-industrialization and, 92
textile industry, 182
Thatcher, Margaret, 224, 225
third industrial revolution, 38–39, 93
Third Sector (public-service enterprises),
        101–136
    abandonment policy for, 106–107, 129
    academic systems in, 129–139
    compensation levels in, 103–104, 111, 112
    components of, 104–105
    defined, 101–102
    employment levels in, 104
    growth in size and complexity, 104, 105
    health-care delivery system in, 124–128
    management in, 105, 107–108, 109–113,
        115–116, 127–128, 129–134, 137–139
    MBAs in, 101, 103
    measurement of performance in, 106,
        109, 116
    as need- versus want-oriented, 106
    productivity in, 19, 111–112, 113
    productivity of capital in, 63, 105
    purposes of institutions in, 106–107
    unionization in, 119–120

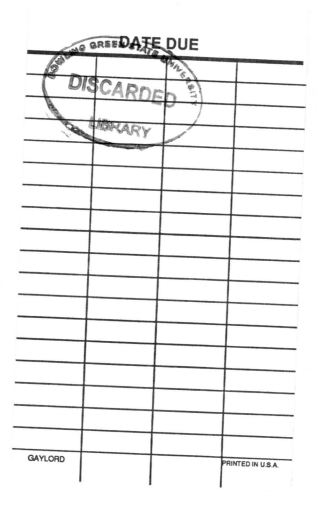